Klaus Griehl

Snakes
Giant Snakes and Non-Venomous Snakes in the Terrarium

Everything about Purchase, Care, Nutrition, and Diseases

With Color Photographs by Outstanding Animal Photographers
and Drawings by Fritz W. Köhler

Barron's

First English language edition published in 1984 by
Barron's Educational Series, Inc.
Third edition 1987
© 1982 by Gräfe and Unzer GmbH, Munich,
West Germany.

The title of the German book is *Schlangen.*

Translated from the German
by Rita and Robert Kimber

All inquiries should be addressed to:
Barron's Educational Series. Inc.
250 Wireless Boulevard
Hauppauge, New York 11788

International Standard Book No. 0-8120-2813-9

Library of Congress Cataloging in Publication Data

Griehl, Klaus.
   Snakes: everything about purchase, care,
nutrition, and diseases.

   Translation of: Schlangen.
   Includes index.

Note and Warning
The subject of this book is the keeping and care of
non-poisonous snakes. Snake keepers should realize,
however, that even the bite of a snake regarded as nonpoisonous can have harmful consequences (see pages
7, 8, and 30). So see a doctor immediately after any
snake bite.

   Handling giant serpents requires a lot of experience
and a great sense of responsibility. Carelessness can be
deadly! Inexperienced snake keepers and snake keepers
who have small children are therefore urgently advised
not to keep giant serpents (see page 9).

   Electrical appliances (see page 30) used in the care
of snakes must carry a valid "UL approved" marking.

Everyone using such equipment should be aware of the
dangers involved with it. It is strongly recommended
that you purchase a device that will instantly shut off
the electrical current in the event of failure in the
appliances or wiring. A circuit-protection device with
a similar function has to be installed by a licensed
electrician.

Front cover: Asian Chicken Snake *(Elaphe
                  oxycephala)*
Back Cover: (Above left) Green Python
                  (Chondropython viridis); (above
                  right) Corn Snake *(Elaphe guttata)*;
                  (below left) Rainbow Boa *(Epicrates
                  cenchria)*; (below right) Common
                  Garter Snake *(Thamnophis sirtalis)*
Inside Front Cover: Reticulate Python *(Python
                  reticulatus)*
Inside Back Cover: Aesculapian Snake *(Elaphe
                  longissima)*

Photographs

Angermayer / Ziesler: Back cover (above left), page
       18
Bechtel: Page 63 (below)
Dossenbach: Inside back cover, back cover (below
       left), page 63 (above)
Essman: Pages 17 (above right), 54
Glader: Page 17 (below left)
Griehl: Page 53 (above right, center right, below
       left)
Hirsch: Page 64 (above left)
R. König: Back cover (above right), pages 17
       (center left), 53 (center left), 64 (center
       left, below left)
Müller: Front cover, pages 36 (above), 64 (center
       right)
Münker: Page 17 (below right)
Progscha: Page 64 (below right)
Reinhard: Inside front cover, back cover (below
       right), pages 17 (above left, center
       right), 35, 64 (above right)
Weber: Page 53 (above left, below right)
Zeininger: Page 36 (below)

PRINTED IN HONG KONG
123   490   13 12

Contents

Preface

In my youth, I spent a lot of my free time going to areas near my home town where there were amphibians and reptiles to be found. With a little knowledge about the habits of these creatures, anyone could easily find their haunts and observe them. Of course I was occasionally tempted to keep some of these creatures in a terrarium, but the captivity of the frogs, toads, salamanders, and snakes I sometimes caught never lasted long. I would soon release them to freedom again. Then, as now, I preferred to see wild creatures in their natural habitat rather than in a cage.

In our day it has become more difficult for a nature lover to observe our native amphibians and reptiles in the wild. The natural habitat of our snakes, for instance, has been reduced to a few small refuges, and even these are crowded on weekends and during vacation time with people in search of recreation. It is hardly surprising, then, that in an attempt to make up for these lost opportunities, people are more and more eager to have "a piece of nature" in their homes.

The pioneer work in developing miniature habitats suited for keeping amphibians and reptiles in captivity was done by aquarium hobbyists, who were the first to set up terrariums. Now the number of amateurs interested in keeping amphibians and reptiles is steadily growing. It is quite amazing how popular snakes have become, these creatures that for thousands of years were considered mysterious and frightening in many cultures.

In this new volume in the series of pet owner's guides, I should like to provide enough knowledge about the habits of snakes to allow you to keep them in a manner that is appropriate to their nature. Before bringing home a snake, you should carefully read the important, though perhaps not very appealing, sections on raising food for snakes (page 41) and on the dangers of keeping giant serpents and poisonous snakes (page 10). In the special chapter "Understanding Snakes," I tell you about the snake's evolution, its amazing capacity for adapting to different environments, its mechanism of locomotion, its sensory organs, its diet, how it captures its prey, and how it reproduces. These are all essential subjects if you want to acquire some insight into the nature of these interesting creatures.

The descriptions of individual species, which take up the better part of this volume, owe much to Dr. Schleich of Munich, who has many years of experience in maintaining terrariums as well as in observing snakes in their natural environment. I should like to take this opportunity to express my special thanks for his generous assistance in the project. The descriptions contain detailed information that is important for keeping snakes. You will find temperature and humidity requirements of different snakes, what kinds of food a particular snake eats, and how the interior of the terrarium should be planned. The descriptions also include some information on the behavioral patterns of individual species and their ways of catching prey in the wild.

In conclusion I should like to express my gratitude to Dr. Gruber of Munich for helping me locate important literature and for providing me with advice whenever it was needed. I also want to thank Fritz W. Köhler whose drawings do much to clarify what is involved in keeping snakes.

Klaus Griehl

Eight Questions for the Future Keeper of Snakes

Before you set out to buy a snake—let alone several—you should seriously ask yourself whether you are able to provide it with the kind of living conditions that will insure the animal's well-being. Remember that if your hobby becomes a burden to you, your animals are bound to suffer, too. The following list of questions will alert you to problems that might arise. If you are unable to answer any of the questions, you should, in your own interest, consult the pertinent chapters of this book. At the end of each question, a page number is given that indicates where the topic at issue is discussed.

• Does your lease allow you to have pets? (Regulations on keeping snakes, Page 21)
• Might you be violating state or federal laws for wildlife protection by keeping the snake you have chosen? (Protected snake species, Page 77)
• Is the snake you want to keep subject to the regulations contained in the Washington Convention of 1976? (The Washington Convention, Page 77)
• Are you able to provide proper conditions for wintering over your snake, particularly if it is of the hibernating kind? (Hibernation, Page 37)
• Terrariums and accessories are fairly expensive even if you build some of the items yourself. For the sake of your snakes' well-being you should not try to save money by cutting corners and doing without modern technical equipment. (The costs of keeping snakes, Page 22, and basic rules for keeping and caring for snakes, Page 31)

• Snakes feed almost entirely on other animals. Will you be able to provide adequate food? (Obtaining food and feeding snakes, Page 41)
• How do you feel about killing small animals or watching your snake do it? Not everyone is able to kill mice, hamsters, or fish; many feel personally responsible for their deaths. Examine yourself carefully to find out how much this would weigh on your conscience. Remember that keeping a terrarium can turn into a nightmare if you routinely have to do something against which your whole inner self rebels. (Obtaining food and feeding snakes, Page 41)
• Terrariums and snakes have to be checked and taken care of daily. Are you prepared to devote a major part of your free time to this hobby? (Basic rules for keeping and caring for snakes, Page 31)

Understanding Snakes

Man's Attitudes Toward Snakes

Environmentalists who fight to save mammals and birds from extinction can count on the wholehearted approval and praise of their fellow citizens. Nobody would dream of criticizing them; after all, they labor in the cause of warm-blooded creatures we all know—attractive fur-bearing or feathered creatures—some of which even please us with their songs. If those same environmentalists were to admit that they are exerting themselves on behalf of amphibians and reptiles, their efforts might even today meet with displeasure and lack of understanding rather than appreciation. Sometimes one still runs into attitudes reminiscent of the Dark Ages, such as the superstition that the ancestors of these "cold-blooded" creatures were in league with the devil.

Snakes use their deeply forked tongues to gather information about the world around them.

A lot of people have a profound antipathy toward snakes. The snake's habit of hiding, its practically noiseless way of moving, and its habit of staring, which is said to have a hypnotic effect, all contribute to the impression that snakes are sinister and dangerous beasts. And because, in the course of evolution, some snakes have developed effective poison glands and fangs to aid them in hunting and in self-defense—weapons that can be dangerous to man as well—the whole "brood of adders and vipers" is subject to merciless persecution and eradication. Nothing that has any resemblance to a snake has a chance against this destructive zeal, not even our European blindworm *(Anguis fragilis),* which, being a limbless lizard, is totally harmless to man.

Division into "Venomous" and "Non-Venomous" Snakes

This book does not describe poisonous snakes or recommend that anyone keep one as a pet. That is why it is important to make a few remarks here on the systematic classification of snakes and on the dangers involved in keeping poisonous snakes and even some so-called "nonpoisonous" ones.

Scientists divide snakes into four groups on the basis of the structure of the teeth:

Harmless Snakes *(Aglypha)*

These snakes have smooth and evenly formed teeth that lack grooves through which poison can be injected into a victim. These snakes are generally considered harmless, and they are the only kinds of snakes listed in the descriptions of individual species (Page 50). But it should be mentioned that in the last few years, isolated cases have been reported in which bites from various snakes in this group have produced symptoms of poisoning. As we now know, even our Common Water Snake and Smooth Snake have some venom in their saliva. George Mamonov of Kiev reported in 1976 that several attendants had suffered ill effects from bites from the supposedly nonpoisonous *Coluber ravergieri*. The reactions varied considerably in different individuals, ranging from no pathological symptoms whatsoever to signs of poisoning accompanied by headaches, pain in the lymph nodes, swelling of the bite wound, and acute pain, lasting for several days in the area of the bite. Mamonov suspects that the reaction to bites depends on the constitution of the individual involved as well as on the size of the snake and the amount of saliva that enters the body of the victim through the wound. In 1978, Dr. Heinz Wermuth also cautioned against the careless handling of "harmless" snakes. In support of his warning he cites the case, described by the authors Mittleman and Goris, of a Japanese snake catcher who died as a result of being bitten by a *Rhabdophis tigrinus*.

The lesson for those of us who have terrariums is, then, to be extremely careful in handling even so-called harmless snakes so that we do not endanger ourselves or others.

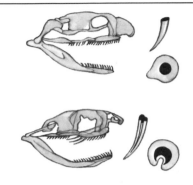

Types of teeth in poisonous and nonpoisonous snakes:
Above: Aglypha have smooth teeth with no channels in them.
Below: The channeled teeth of mildly poisonous snakes (opisthoglypha) are set well back in jaws and are linked to poison glands.

Mildly Poisonous or Rear-Fanged Snakes (Opisthoglypha)

In those snakes the hindmost teeth of the upper jaw are grooved and much enlarged. They are connected to venom glands and thus act as poison fangs. Because they are so far back in the mouth, accidental bites are rare, but the danger of fatal poisoning is nevertheless far greater than in the case of snakes belonging to the *aglypha* group. Two of the foremost herpetologists of our time were killed by mildly poisonous snakes. Dr. Karl Patterson Schmidt died in 1957 after being bitten by an African Boomslang *(Dispholidus typus),* and Professor Robert Mertens succumbed to the bite of the rear-fanged *Thelotornis kirtlandii.*

Understanding Snakes

You are therefore strongly advised to keep away from mildly poisonous snakes, no matter how warmly pet dealers or other terrarium enthusiasts may recommend them as "harmless" pets.

Elapine and Marine Snakes *(Proteroglypha)*

These snakes have a pair of permanently erect, enlarged fangs in the front of the upper jaw. The fangs have a deep, almost fully enclosed vertical groove through which the venom is injected when the snake bites. The *Elapidae* family, including cobras, mambas, and coral snakes, and the *Hydrophiidae* family, or sea snakes, make up this group.

Vipers and Pit Vipers *(Solenoglypha)*

These snakes have two or more large fangs at the front of their upper jaws. The fangs are attached to movable bones which swing the fangs out at a right angle to the jaw bone when the snake gets ready to attack. The fangs are canaliculate (i.e., they have a hollow canal running through them) and act like hypodermic needles. The orifice is at the very tip of the fang for effective transmission of the venom. These snakes include the *Viperidae* family with its two subfamilies, the Viperinae, to which the Common Viper, the Gaboon Viper, and the Puff Adder belong, and the Crotalinae, i.e., the pit vipers, to which the Fer-de-lance and the rattlesnakes belong.

I want to warn emphatically against keeping highly poisonous snakes such as

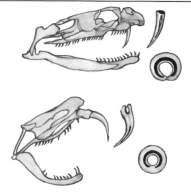

Above: Proteroglypha have large frontal fangs equipped with almost entirely enclosed channels that carry poison.
Below: Solenoglypha have hollow fangs that swing forward when the snake bites and function like hypodermic needles to inject the poison.

the ones mentioned in the last two paragraphs. Snake enthusiasts who insist on keeping these animals in their homes display a shocking irresponsibility, not only toward themselves, but also toward their fellow human beings. Nobody can reasonably claim that he or she can foresee and prevent everything that might lead to an accident. I have over the years gotten to know several keepers of poisonous snakes, and in my opinion most of them handle their pets with a carelessness I find hard to comprehend. Almost all of them felt compelled to prove to me how tame their pets were, and even my most eloquent protests could not stop them from displaying their snakes to me "in the wilds of the living room." I must admit that my fear has kept me from paying any of these people a second visit. What I find even more shocking is that

Understanding Snakes

hardly any of these amateur herpetologists had an antivenomous serum for treating bites by their particular snakes. The only legitimate reason I can see for keeping poisonous snakes in captivity is the scientific one of developing new and more effective medications through pharmacological research.

Some Thoughts on the Subject of Keeping Giant Serpents

Some especially passionate advocates of keeping poisonous snakes may object that this book does list dangerous species as possible pets—namely, a number of giant serpents. I finally decided to include some of these species in my descriptions only after long deliberation. The reason that finally swayed me is that many baby snakes offered for sale by pet stores belong to these species of giant snakes. These young snakes at this stage in their lives are no thicker than a ball point pen and therefore harmless; they are popular and sell quickly. The problems show up soon, however, because young giant snakes grow extremely fast. They outgrow their original terrariums in no time at all and then have to be moved to larger ones. Giant snakes, as everyone knows, squeeze their victims to death; they quickly reach a size where they can not only seriously hurt but even kill their keepers. According to one newspaper, a Boa Constrictor barely more than eight feet long (250 cm) killed its tamer, Jean-Guy Leclaire. Another snake that was considerably smaller bit a snake enthusiast so badly that one-half of his face will be permanently disfigured. I could go on listing publicly reported mishaps at some length but will instead simply reiterate once more and emphatically that handling snakes carelessly can and often does result in tragedy.

Short Introduction to Snakes

If you want to keep snakes in a terrarium, you should have some basic knowledge of the evolution, peculiarities, and way of life of this class of animals. This will give you some clues about how the snakes in your care should be treated. Our short introduction to snakes is meant as a basis on which the reader can build. By exchanging notes with other amateur herpetologists and by reading specialized literature, one can gradually accumulate a solid stock of knowledge concerning the life and habits of these pets.

Snakes in Myth and History

In myths and legends all over the world, serpents play a significant part. In Mexico, the serpent god Quetzalcoatl was considered the god of life. To Aesculapius, the Greek god of healing, the snake's periodic shedding of its skin was a symbol of constant rejuvenation. Greek mythology also includes the story of Typhon and Echidna, creatures whose lower bodies were those of serpents and who bred monsters. Egyptian gods and royalty carried the symbol of the asp on their foreheads, and the Byzantine bishops had a snake on their scepters as an emblem of wisdom. In India, offerings are made even today to the cobra, which stands for the Hindu god Siva. The Hopi Indians used to perform ritual dances with rattlesnakes, and even in our modern world, the staff of Aesculapius is recognized as the symbol of medicine.

Evolutionary Origins of Snakes

Relatively little is known about the early history of snakes, but fossil deposits found seem to indicate that snakes roamed the earth together with other reptiles and saurians as early as 180 million years ago. We do know for a fact that snakes arose from a lizard ancestor and that these lizards went through a long evolutionary process during which their bodies gradually became elongated while the limbs became more and more rudimentary. Some scientists believe that the earless monitor lizard *Lanthanotus,* which is found on Borneo, represents a modern version of the missing link between lizards and snakes. Snakes thus "lost their legs" in the course of their evolution. This surely would not have happened had it not been necessary for survival and proved advantageous in competing with rivals for food. The presence of some lizard-like features in older and often more

"primitive" snakes, such as the boas and pythons, further supports this theory of evolution of serpents. The skeletons of these snakes still show vestigial pelvic bones and anal spurs that represent the remnants of hind legs. These remnants of legs have, of course, lost all function in locomotion. It is likely that they are used by the male to stimulate the female during copulation. In the more modern, or "higher," snakes of the Colubridae, Viperidae, and Hydrophiidae families, this feature is absent.

Adaptability

Their extraordinary adaptability to extreme environmental conditions has enabled snakes to become established in almost all areas of the earth except for the polar regions and the great depths of lakes and oceans. Snakes occur with greater frequency, of course, in areas where the climate is most suitable to them, i.e., the warmer zones. The number of species diminishes drastically as the climate gets colder and the environment more inhospitable. The Common Viper and the Garter Snake are best adapted to harsh living conditions. They are found almost as far north as the Arctic Circle, while one member of the family of pit vipers has penetrated as far south in Argentina as the fiftieth degree of latitude. The record for altitude is held by the Himalayan Moccasin, which has been found at elevations of almost 16,000 feet (5,000 m).

Understanding Snakes

Locomotion of Snakes

Although there are some minor differences in the body structure of different kinds of snakes, the method of locomotion is basically the same for all of them. We usually describe a snake's way of moving as "serpentine." The wave-like forward motion is accomplished by the repeated contraction and relaxation of muscles. In this way the snake can push against small irregularities in the surface over which it is moving. This pushing or traction provides the force necessary for forward motion. If you placed a snake on a completely smooth piece of glass, it would be unable to move away because it would have nothing to get a grip on. Marine snakes make use of the same principle of pushing against resistance when they swim in wide horizontal curves close to the surface of the water. In response to the special conditions of their habitat, some species have developed variations in their basic method of locomotion. Probably the most interesting of these is a process called "sidewinding." Some desert snakes make use of this special technique. They loop their bodies sideways across the sand, touching the ground only in a few places with the belly side. The body rises up and makes a loop that starts behind the head and reaches to the base of the tail; then the snake tosses itself sideways, touching the ground with different sections of its body, rather like a person does putting his right and left foot down alternately.

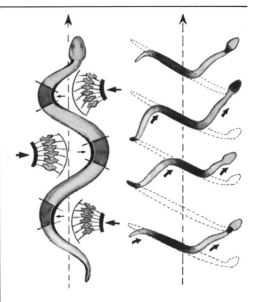

Snake locomotion. Left: The "serpentine" motion, in which the snake exerts pressure on irregularities in the earth's surface by tensing and relaxing its muscles.
Right: "Sidewinding," a means of locomotion that some desert snakes use for moving on loose sand. The snake moves sideways along the ground.

The speed with which snakes move is usually greatly exaggerated in reports of encounters with them. They can, of course, move faster than a person on uneven terrain, but experiments have shown that even the fastest snakes can barely reach a speed of 4 miles per hour (6 km/h). The record is held by a mamba which achieved a speed of 6.5 mph (10.6 km/h) over a distance of 47 yards (43 m).

Understanding Snakes

Sensory Organs

Sensory capacities of snakes vary with their way of life, specialization, and method of adaptation to their environment. Snakes are not able to regulate their body temperature; the degree of their activity thus depends on the temperature of their surroundings.

Snakes Lack Organs of Hearing

Snakes lack not only external ears but also inner ear canals and tympanic membranes. They are therefore unable to perceive sounds. To make up for this, they are capable of registering even very slight vibrations, such as the ones created by the footsteps of a person.

The Eyes and Their "Hypnotic" Stare

With the exception of the burrowing species, snakes generally have well-developed vision. However, they recognize only moving objects and are probably unable to perceive shapes as such. Many people believe even today that snakes hypnotize their prey with their stare. This theory has, of course, long been disproved. Mice, rats, and other vertebrates that were placed in a terrarium together with snakes paid no attention to the predators as long as the snakes remained motionless. But as soon as the snakes started to move, the other animals responded with fright. Probably the snake's motionless stare gave rise to the myth of its hypnotic abilities. But this stare is the result of an anatomical peculiarity. To keep the eyes clean, the snake's eyelids have become modified and have grown together into solid, transparent caps somewhat like the curved glass over the face of a wrist watch. This covering of the eyes consists of a horny layer of skin and is vulnerable to mechanical injury and to wear and tear. This horny layer is replaced by a new one when the snake sheds the rest of its skin.

Sense of Smell

Its excellent sense of smell is the snake's most important tool in taking in the world. In most people's minds, the word "snake" probably evokes images of serpentine movement and of the tongue flicking in and out of the mouth. The deeply forked, two-pronged tongue emerges through a space beneath the nose shield. The mouth does not have to be open. The tongue absorbs the olfactory elements of the air, and when it retracts, the data it has gathered about the environment is passed on to the Jacobson's organ, a region of chemically sensitive nerve endings in the roof of the mouth, where this information is evaluated.

Size and Rate of Growth

If you encounter a snake in the wild, it is almost impossible to estimate its length accurately. In an attempt to escape and remain undetected, the snake will try to stay in hiding, and only parts of its body will be visible at any one time. That is why old reports about the size of giant serpents should be taken with a grain of salt. On some expeditions, anacondas about 50 feet (16 m) long were supposedly sighted, but to this day, no anaconda as much as 33 feet (10 m) long has actually been captured, even though the New York Zoological Society many years ago offered $5,000 to anyone who could procure a specimen this large. However, in captivity, the Giant Anaconda sometimes grows to about 30 feet (9 m). In some rare cases the Reticulate Python has reached a length of over 33 feet (10 m). But these giants among snakes are exceptions, and apart from the two species mentioned, only the Indian Python *(Python molurus),* the Rock Python *(P. sebae),* and the Amethyst Python *(P. amethystinus)* reach lengths of over 20 feet (6 m). The chapter describing individual species of snakes includes more specific information on record lengths.

There is one fact we should be aware of. In contrast to other vertebrate creatures, whose growth usually stops when sexual maturity is reached, snakes keep growing. The rate at which they grow depends on several factors. Baby snakes start out growing quite fast, leaving behind as quickly as possible the critical phase when they are a ready prey to other animals. Snakes that hibernate grow very slowly, if at all, during hibernation. Finally, the rate of growth depends on the availability of food, which, in the wild, is dependent on the conditions of the environment.

How Long Do Snakes Live?

It is hard to say anything definite about the life expectancy of snakes in the wild. Our information is based primarily on the reports of herpetologists and terrarium buffs who have held snakes in captivity. According to this information a Giant Anaconda can live up to twenty-eight years, a Rock Python, twenty years, a Corn Snake, twenty-one years, and a Milk Snake, eighteen years. It is conceivable that anacondas and the Indian Python may live up to fifty or sixty years, perhaps even longer. Since snakes keep growing as long as they live, large specimens of a given species are always relatively old.

Food and the Catching of Prey

Snakes Are Meat Eaters

All snakes are carnivorous, but depending on their species, the prey ranges from small insects to fairly large mammals. Some snakes are so specialized in their feeding habits that they depend entirely on one kind of animal in their habitat. Water snakes feed primarily on amphibians and fish; arboreal species usually eat birds, and ground dwelling snakes are very useful pest control agents because they consume small rodents. Some species, as (for example) the members of the *Lampropeltis* genus, even eat other snakes. The African Egg-eating Snake represents a case of unusual specialization in diet. As its name indicates, this snake lives exclusively on eggs. The well-known Dutch photographer Arend van den Nieuwenhuizen has recorded this unique eating procedure on film, and his series of photographs strikes even an experienced snake keeper (who is used to the normal swallowing feats of snakes) as an amazing document. When one considers the difference in size between the egg and the snake's head, it seems utterly impossible that the upper and lower jaws could distend enough to reach around the egg. Nieuwenhuizen reports that it takes almost one-half hour from the time the snake gets ready to eat until the moment when the egg actually disappears inside the snake's mouth. There are other authenticated reports of the exceptional swallowing capacities of

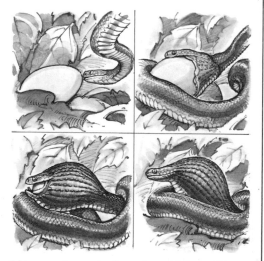

The egg-eating snake devouring a bird egg. The process of swallowing, shown here in four pictures, is a long and arduous task that can take up to half an hour.

different snakes. In one case, a leopard was found inside the stomach of an eighteen-foot (5.5 m) Reticulate Python.

Hunting the Prey

Snakes use different methods of hunting and killing their prey. The Ringed Snake *(Natrix natrix)* lives entirely on unarmed creatures such as frogs and fish. It has therefore no need to kill its prey first but simply starts eating it alive after getting ahold of it. Snakes hunting animals that could hurt them proceed differently. A rat, for instance, must not be given the chance to use its strong teeth in defense. Some water snakes and pythons therefore wrap themselves around their prey and quickly squeeze it to death. Poisonous snakes, vipers, and pit vipers inject a paralyzing or deadly venom so fast that the human eye is incapable of actually seeing the process of biting. The snake gets away from the scene of danger within fractions of a second and then calmly awaits the effects of the venom.

Swallowing and Lathering Up

A snake ordinarily swallows its prey head first. This way the hairs or feathers of the victim lie down flat rather than stand up and block the way. In addition, the prey is lathered with saliva to insure smooth passage. No snake is able to break its prey into pieces with the help of its teeth. Instead, snakes have highly effective stomach juices that help digest the entire victim—bones, horny tissue, sinews, hair, and all.

The Digestive Process

Since snakes are cold-blooded and cannot regulate their body temperature, the speed at which the digestive process takes place depends on the external temperature. Also, fish and amphibians, which are "light" foods, are digested more quickly than warm-blooded mammals. After eating, snakes retire to resting places that offer protection and preferred temperatures. Usually they do not become active again until their previous meal is fully digested and the remains are excreted. Some snakes, especially the giant ones, fast for long periods between meals. This may be because a huge amount of food is taken in with literally one swallow. Giant snakes that are held in captivity sometimes go without eating for months without significant weight loss. The reason for this is probably that they have been previously overfed, over a period of time.

Intervals between Feedings

If you are keeping baby snakes in your terrarium, it is best to offer them food once a week. For adult colubrid snakes a feeding every two weeks is sufficient, and giant snakes can be offered a plentiful meal every three to four weeks without fear that they might suffer from hunger in between.

Be Careful Not to Overfeed

It is always better to err in the direction of underfeeding snakes than to give in to anxieties of starving them and consequently feeding them too much. Experience has shown that too much food has an adverse effect on the longevity and the reproductive vigor of these animals.

The Molt

Snakes keep growing as long as they live. In this growth, cells of the deeper layers of the skin are constantly produced and provide a protective keratinous layer on the surface of the body. Since this layer cannot expand indefinitely, it has to be sloughed off periodically and replaced by a new one. The first sign that the snake is getting ready to shed its skin is that the whole body takes on a visible milky opaqueness. This opaqueness is particularly visible in the otherwise very clear eyes of the snake. After a few days, this opaqueness disappears, and the snake begins to rub its snout vigorously against hard objects to try to break the skin. When this has happened, it likes to crawl through a narrow crack or space to help peel off the old skin. The skin comes off inside out, like a tight glove, starting at the head and ending with the tip of the tail. In terrarium inhabitants, the smooth functioning of the shedding process (when the entire skin is cast off in one piece) is a sign that the snake is in good health.

Reproduction

Behavior during Mating Season
The mating of snakes is limited to certain periods that are determined by environmental factors in the habitat of any given species. As a rule, snakes that are normally solitary in their habits set out in search of a partner, after emerging from their winter rest. In some species, combat dances have been observed in which the dominance of one individual is established. Most species engage in lengthy courtship games. Glands in the skin emit olfactory particles that help the sexes recognize each other. The male is the active and visibly more excited party, as it seeks to get in physical contact with the female. The female responds by twitching her raised, forward-pointing body and often by rattling or beating her tail.

Two male, non-poisonous snakes in a combat dance (see, too, the drawing on the title page).

Copulation
In the course of courting, the male tries to place his cloaca next to that of the female. As soon as he succeeds, he introduces a hemipenis into the female's cloaca. (The male's copulatory organ is made up of two mirror-image "hemipenises.") Now actual copulation begins, and it may last for several hours or even days because the hemipenis is covered with spinelike protrusions and becomes firmly lodged inside the female. During this period the male follows every movement of the female, and in some species he also holds on to her by biting her neck.

Gestation
After mating, the snakes separate and resume their solitary lives. In some species, the females refrain from all food intake for the entire period of gestation. This is rather remarkable, considering that, depending on the species, gestation can last anywhere from thirty to well over one hundred days.

Laying Eggs and Incubation
Most snakes lay eggs, depositing them in protected places. Many species then abandon the eggs, but there are exceptions. The best known of these are some pythons, which not only stay with the eggs and coil themselves around them to protect them, but can also raise the air temperature by several degrees by rhythmically contracting the muscles in their

19

bodies. But even in these cases, the care for the young ends as soon as they hatch. Once they leave the eggs, the hatchlings are on their own.

Live-Bearers

Some snakes give birth to live young. Among these are the boas, the European Smooth Snake, and most vipers and pit vipers. This method has the advantage that the fate of the eggs is not left to chance. They spend the entire incubation period protected inside the maternal body. The mother snake always strives to achieve optimal temperatures by basking in the sun, and the young benefit from this. Some snakes even delay the birth of the young during inclement weather conditions. The Common Viper, for instance, can postpone birth past winter to the climatically more favorable spring. In ovoviviparous species like these, the young break out of the eggs inside the maternal body or in the process of birth and enter the world as miniature snakes fully equipped with all the functions and behavioral patterns of the species.

Baby Snakes

Soon after birth, the young snakes shed their skins and then embark on their first "hunting expeditions." Baby snakes are a favorite food of many other animals and it is crucial for them to grow and leave this stage behind fast. That is why their need for food is large in comparison to that of adult snakes.

Considerations Before You Buy

Regulations You Must Observe

Before you decide to buy a snake, you should reread your lease to check whether it contains a clause that forbids you to keep pets. If this is the case, your landlord is unlikely to make an exception because prejudice against snakes is prevalent and hard to overcome. If your lease does not explicitly prohibit the keeping of pets, there is no legal basis for discriminating against snakes as long as they are nonpoisonous and no more than ten feet (3 m) long. But you should make very sure that your snakes are housed in escape-proof containers, because a snake that makes an unexpected appearance in the hall or on a neighbor's balcony will be regarded as a nuisance and an imposition on other tenants, and may be cause for termination of your lease.

Also make sure before you buy a snake that it does not belong to a protected species (page 77) that may not be bought or sold.

Where to Buy a Snake

Pet dealers are business people, and their stock reflects the demands of the public. It is therefore not surprising that they carry primarily mammals, birds, and fish, for which there is a ready market. Snakes are usually found in pet stores only if the owner has a personal interest in them or is himself an amateur herpetologist. But any pet dealer will be happy to use his contacts in helping you locate the snake you have your heart set on. Take your time and visit all the pet stores in your area. Do not skip the pet sections of large department stores because their inventories often include reptiles as show pieces. If your search is still unsuccessful, procure copies of aquarium and terrarium magazines, which usually appear monthly. Here you will find not only ads by dealers specializing in terrarium pets but also notices placed by hobbyists trying to sell the offspring of their pets. Do not spare time and money at this point, but go to see the owner of the snakes for sale and have a good look at the animals yourself.

Never Choose a Sick Snake

In large-scale establishments it unfortunately sometimes happens that lots of animals are crowded together in small containers because of lack of space. If this is the case, be sure to examine your snake thoroughly. External injuries usually heal quickly, but they often leave ugly scars. Never buy an animal with an oozing wound because you usually cannot tell whether it is the result of a harmless injury or a case of *mycosis,* a rather serious fungus infection. In no case should you buy a snake with mouth rot. Even terrarium experts have a hard time combatting this disease. Buying weakened animals is an unsound proposition even if the dealer offers you a special low price for them. Medications for treating sick snakes are not inexpensive, and weakened animals often refuse all food and finally die.

The Cost of Keeping Snakes

The price of snakes depends on a number of factors, and it is impossible to give specific amounts that are in any sense binding. Generally speaking, young snakes are cheaper than grown ones. Dealers often figure the price according to the length of a snake. Thus a Boa Constrictor 40 inches (100 cm) long might cost $50 and another 60 inches (150 cm) long would be $75. Of course, the price is also affected by how rare a snake is. Some snakes, such as the *Elaphe obsoleta,* which, in recent years, has been bred successfully in large numbers, can often be bought for as little as $10. Other species such as the *Chondropython viridis* or the *Aspidites melanocephalus* may command well over $500. The terrarium represents another not inconsiderable investment. A well-built model measuring 78 × 17 × 20 inches (200 × 42.5 × 50 cm) would, in the United States, cost about $375 without accessories. You would have to figure $50 to $85 more, depending on the model, for lighting and cover. The rest of the accessories, including heater and thermostat, would cost approximately another $50. The cost of electricity for

As this drawing shows, the terrarium can be a decorative addition to your living space without being any less practical.

lighting and heating the terrarium depends on the temperature of the room where the terrarium is located. Of course, you can save considerably on initial costs if you build your own terrarium or buy a kit and put it together yourself. Such kits have recently been advertised by various manufacturers in magazines aimed at terrarium buffs.

Getting the Snake Home

Do not go off to buy a snake without first giving some thought to how you will bring it home. After all, you cannot simply stick it in your pocket. Take along some strong linen sacks of different sizes that can be tied shut and do not have any holes. The dealer will have packing material, but it may have been used before, and this increases the danger of introducing some disease into your own terrarium. The trip home will be a strain for your snake under the best of circumstances, but you can save it some stress by moving it as gently as possible. Styrofoam boxes are very practical for this purpose. You can place the bag with the snake inside in the box and thus protect the animal to some extent from temperature changes en route. I would advise anyone who intends to keep snakes in a terrarium to get in touch with a herpetological society (addresses, page 78) or to become a member of such an organization. Some of these groups publish lists of terrarium animals that members want to sell or swap. In addition, you will

receive a complete list of members as well as addresses of the various local sections that are headed by experienced herpetologists. Contact with other members is helpful, and you will always have someone to call on when you most need advice.

Getting the Terrarium Ready

You will want to have a functioning container set up and ready before you buy your snake. Most terrarium buffs who already have a sizable snake colony always keep a quarantine container ready for new snakes. It should be kept separate from the occupied terrariums, preferably in a different room. This precaution largely eliminates the danger that a new snake might introduce some undetected disease into the established population. Novices will do well to imitate this practice of the experts and house their new purchase in an easily surveyable quarantine container for observation during the first couple of weeks. Now that you know the size of your snake and have informed yourself through appropriate literature and conversations with other hobbyists what its requirements are, you will have enough time to set up a terrarium that allows the snake to live a comfortable existence and that satisfies your aesthetic sense as well.

Selecting and Equipping
the Terrarium

In response to the growing demand of the last few years, pet supply stores now offer a fairly wide variety of ready-made terrariums. For a number of snakes, these containers are perfectly adequate. Young snakes in particular and species that do not grow to a large size can be housed in these commercially available terrariums without suffering. Things begin to become problematic if we intend to keep snakes that have specific environmental demands. Snakes that live primarily in trees in their natural habitat have to be offered opportunities for climbing in captivity. For them, a tall terrarium is obviously more suitable than a low one with a large floor area. This latter type would, on the other hand, be appropriate for ground dwelling or burrowing snakes. In many cases, building your own terrarium is the best solution.

A Homemade Terrarium

Fish fanciers were the first to construct tanks by glueing glass panels together without frames. In recent years this method has been adopted for terrariums as well as aquariums. These terrariums look elegant in a living room, but they have a disadvantage; they can only be used as single units. If you want to expand your setup later, you cannot stack them, as you can the wide, solid glass terrariums held together by metal frames, or trays made of wood or artificial materials. Any hardware store carries angle irons which can be cut to the desired size

and welded together. If you are not exceptionally skillful yourself, you should leave this job to an expert, because unless the frames are welded together at exactly the right angle, there is no guarantee that the glass panels will fit tightly in place. All metal parts should be rustproofed before you proceed to the next step. To allow as much light to enter the terrarium as possible, it is best to use wood or other opaque material only for the bottom and the back wall. The other panels should be made of glass. Most artificial materials require no treatment against decay, but wood should be protected against moisture with a special water-

A standard homemade terrarium. The sliding doors are mounted in tracks. The floor guard holds the lower track for the sliding glass doors and keeps the bottom material from falling out of the terrarium. The upper guard serves as a mount for the upper track and prevents annoying light from the terrarium illumination from coming out into the room. The heating coil is laid under the sand.

proof coating. If you want to be able to get into the terrarium easily to do the necessary chores, you should install sliding glass panels at the front. These panels are mounted in tracks available in either metal or plastic.

How Big Should the Terrarium Be?

Most snakes feel no great need to move around. It is therefore hard to recommend specific sizes for terrariums. Everybody has to develop an individual sense or intuition in this matter. I have had a Boa Constrictor five feet long (150 cm) for which a terrarium measuring 48 × 32 × 28 inches (120 × 80 × 70 cm) was quite sufficient. A tree dwelling *Elaphe oxycephala* measuring about 36 inches (90 cm) lived for a long time in a container 24 × 32 × 32 inches (60 × 80 × 80 cm). Six *Elaphe obsoleta quadrivittata* housed together in a terrarium of 52 × 32 × 32 inches (130 × 80 × 80 cm) for three years not only grew to respectable sizes but also mated and made me the foster parent of forty-three baby snakes.

Different Possibilities for Heating

Since snakes cannot regulate their body temperature, we have to provide them with the temperatures they need in order to thrive. We have to be especially careful when we heat a small terrarium because it can quickly overheat. To prevent this, the heater must be connected to a thermostat. In small indoor terrariums, I have successfully used rod type aquarium heaters. Buried in a heat-conducting compound that is not soluble in water, they provided enough heat to warm the bottom, and the heated bottom was sought out by the snakes after their meals. Larger terrariums, in which only part of the bottom area should be heated, can be placed on heating pads. Such heating pads, encased in waterproof covers, are commercially available and usually have a switch with three settings to achieve the desired temperature. In recent years, heating cables with a plastic or metal coating have turned out to be very good for heating terrariums. They

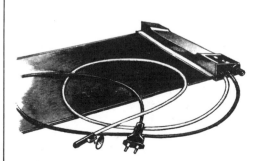

A heating plate is handy for warming several small terrariums from one source of heat (available in pet stores).

Selecting and Equipping the Terrarium

are available at different wattages and, depending on how they are used, they allow us either to heat only certain areas or to create an even warmth over the whole bottom. If you keep tree-dwelling snakes which do not like to spend time on the bottom of the terrarium, you should mount a heating cable on a branch, but in such a manner that the snakes can get away from it if they get too warm. For burrowing snakes, it is necessary to anchor the cables down solidly or to bury them in the heat-conducting compound mentioned previously.

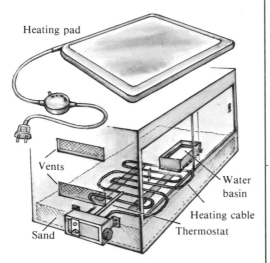

Heating pad

Vents

Water basin

Heating cable

Thermostat

Sand

Heating the terrarium. Heating pads with three temperature settings have proved satisfactory. They are particularly good for snakes that need warm ground in only part of the terrarium. Heating wires have the advantage that they can be placed under the bottom material or wound around branches.

There are still old-time terrarium experts who swear by various home-built rigs using light bulbs for heat. In view of the technically excellent heaters that are available today, I think it is foolish to stick to these primitive methods. Snakes can easily get burned on bulbs even when they are protected by screening. Also, light bulbs are susceptible to breaking if water is splashed on them, and the resulting glass splinters represent an additional hazard for snakes. When setting up and equipping a terrarium, you should never try to save money at the cost of safety.

Ventilation

Unfortunately, the importance of proper ventilation is often overlooked. Inhabitants of a terrarium can thrive only if there is an adequate exchange of gases. To insure this you can utilize the terrarium's heat source. Rising temperatures carry air upward, so by placing vents at appropriate spots, you can make sure that the air will be constantly refreshed. It is advisable to use plastic vents. Hardware stores carry sturdy ones that are suitable for large terrariums. Vents made of various kinds of wire mesh or screening should not be used for snakes because these restless animals push and rub hard against the mesh with their noses in an attempt to find a way out, and they often hurt themselves in the process.

Selecting and Equipping the Terrarium

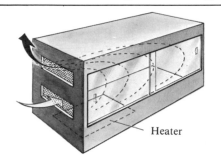

Vents placed in one side of the terrarium and floor heating on the same side provide adequate air exchange. The warm air rises and flows out of the terrarium.

Lighting

Most reptiles love the sun. They need not only its warmth but also its light to feel truly comfortable. In our temperate zones there is not enough light for our exotic charges, even if we place their terrariums next to a window. Providing them with an additional light source is therefore essential. Fluorescent light tubes are ideal for this purpose not only because they use little electricity but also because the light they provide is closer in composition to daylight than other artificial light. Combining a regular fluorescent tube with an ultraviolet tube results in nearly perfect lighting. If you cannot install this combination of tubes, you should shine an ultraviolet heat lamp on your snakes approximately twice a week. Exposure to this light is important for the production of vitamin D in the body. But make sure the animals have a cooler place away from these rays for retreating to, if the temperature gets higher than is comfortable for them.

Fresh Water and Air Humidity

Captive snakes must always have fresh water available. You should install a drinking bowl in such a way that you can remove it and replace it again easily without disturbing the snakes. Since some snakes like to defecate in water, you must clean the drinking bowl regularly to prevent infections. The fresh water should be slightly warmed. Try to use a dish that corresponds to the size of the snake. Not only water snakes like to take day-long baths; other snakes also often spend a lot of time in the water bowl before they shed their skins. Some snakes need a daily sprinkling from a water vaporizer such as the ones used for indoor plants. This is good for raising the humidity inside the terrarium. Also, many snakes drink only reluctantly from bowls; they much prefer to suck up the drops formed by the spray. The enjoyment of the daily spraying was quite obvious among my *Elaphe oxycephala*—snakes that descend to the ground only reluctantly—as they practically gulped down the spray water. Terrarium enthusiasts who like to keep plants in with their snakes should use soft water; otherwise ugly calcium deposits will form on the leaves over time. To check the degree of humidity you should install a hygrometer in the terrarium in an easily visible spot.

Selecting and Equipping the Terrarium

The Bottom Material in the Terrarium

The wrong bottom material can lead to a serious impairment of snakes' health. The basic rule is that we have to be able to check the whole floor area easily to find and remove droppings and thus prevent the danger of infection. For this reason, some terrarium keepers choose to have a perfectly sterile and hygienic terrarium with a bottom that is covered with newspapers or blotting paper. The advantage of this method is that the paper can be changed within a matter of seconds. We may believe that this solution is cheerless and sacrifices everything to efficiency, but the snakes surely do not care. However, since most of us like to display our terrariums and the snakes in it as decorative centerpieces in our living rooms, we do not want them to look like eyesores, and generally reserve this optically unattractive method for quarantine containers.

Peat moss, a mixture of sand and peat, or forest soil mixed with bark, dry leaves, and stones has a natural and attractive look. We should remember, however, that hygiene is of prime importance in keeping snakes, and this kind of bottom material is almost impossible to keep sterile. Droppings are hard to detect in it, and the danger of bacterial growths is great. Fine river sand is a good alternative. I myself and most of the terrarium buffs I know use the white, sterile sand that pet supply stores have for sale. This is the most expensive solution if you look only at the initial cost, but if you consider what you might end up paying if your snakes get sick, it seems the most reasonable alternative. If you inspect your terrarium daily, you are unlikely to overlook droppings in the white sand. Even with burrowing snakes, there is very little danger that excrement will be buried and hidden from sight if you check at frequent intervals.

Decorations

With the exception of the burrowing species, almost all snakes like to climb in a terrarium, even if they spend most of their time on the ground in the wild. Even the spartan advocates of sterile terrariums will equip their snakes' living quarters with a few rocks or other objects to climb on. The rocks you choose should not be too light because some snakes dig underneath them or use the rough spots on them to help in sloughing off the skin. You should not underestimate the strength snakes can display in these activities. And a rock that topples over may shatter a glass panel or kill other inhabitants of the terrarium. It is therefore best to cement several heavy rocks together in such a way that a cave-like retreat is formed, as well as a raised plateau. If you keep tree-dwelling snakes, you will be obliged to install one or several climbing trees. If you collect the materials for this from the woods, you will have to take similar precautions, as in the case of the bottom material, to prevent rotting, (decay involving bacterial activity). This danger always remains

Selecting and Equipping the Terrarium

very high in a hot, humid terrarium climate. The least you can do to minimize the danger is to boil the branches in tap water and disinfect them several times at seven-day intervals with a household disinfectant. Cork tubes that are sold by florists and pet supply dealers make a problem-free and attractive decoration that is practically one hundred percent safe from decay. These tubes are especially useful for installing heating cables and as holders for flower pots. It is often quite difficult to decorate a terrarium with natural branches because they must be solidly attached in at least two places, and this is not always feasible. In recent years, artificial resins have come on the market and are sold at craft supply

stores. If you like to build things yourself and have the necessary skills, you can use these materials to build climbing trees that fit in with the other accessories and are just the right size for your terrarium.

There is no doubt that the back wall plays a crucial role in the aesthetic effect of the whole terrarium, and it is understandable that most terrarium buffs try to achieve optic harmony between this backdrop and the other decorations. I must admit that I am tempted to categorically advise all terrarium enthusiasts to relinquish their aesthetic desires on this point and do without any decorations. A smooth back wall is easy to keep clean, whereas a rough surface is hard to clean. On the other hand, I well remem-

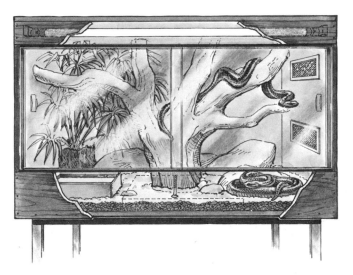

Decorations in a terrarium for giant snakes have to be rugged and heavy. Be sure that the decorations are fastened securely enough that they cannot be moved. The drinking basin should, if possible, be large enough to serve as a bathtub as well.

29

Selecting and Equipping the Terrarium

ber that I myself disregarded this same advice given me by experts. I, too, felt that a "natural" backdrop was well worth the extra care it involved. My first attempt was a decoration composed of pieces of tree bark. I screwed each piece solidly and immovably (according to my notions and to the best of my manual skills) to the back wall. The spaces between the individual pieces were, in my view, so small that at best a just-hatched corn snake might have hidden in them. A Common King Snake *(Lampropeltis getulus holbrooki)* four feet long (120 cm) moved into the terrarium and had by the very next day succeeded in prying up some of the bark pieces and disappeared behind the decoration. I would occasionally have the pleasure of observing it for a few moments on the heated floor. But as soon as it became aware of my presence, it would hide again behind the decoration in a flash. In this way I could keep no tabs on the health of my snake, and I soon decided to dismantle my fancy bark decoration. I ran into similar problems with a terrarium I had equipped with large rock fragments for giant snakes. I had arranged the rocks to form terraces starting in the middle of the terrarium and rising up in steps toward the back wall. The rocks were held together with cement and all cracks filled with a nonpoisonous and nonsoluble filler. This "dry terrarium" looked very decorative when it was new, but keeping it clean was not only a chore but also a regular torture, because bits of excreta and old skin could be removed only with tweezers and with considerable unnatural twistings of the body. Since it is impossible to keep a constant eye on the snakes in the course of this work, I sustained several unpleasant bites, to boot.

Safety is Crucial

It goes without saying that terrariums intended for snakes must be sturdy and tight so the animals cannot escape. The cover and sliding panels must have locks or bolts that close securely because snakes often develop an amazing sixth sense for detecting flaws in their cages.

Furthermore, you have to be aware of the dangers connected with the use of electrical appliances and wiring, so keep these safety tips in mind:

The electrical appliances described in this book must carry a valid "UL approved" mark.

It is highly recommended that you purchase a device (available in pet stores) that will shut off the current if there should be any failure in your appliances or wiring. A circuit-protection device that functions similarly can be installed in your fuse box by a licensed electrician.

Basic Rules for Keeping and Caring for Snakes

Introducing the Snake into Your Home

After you have purchased your snake and brought it home, first leave it in the quarantine container (page 31) for about two weeks for observation. Treat it against ticks and mites even if you see no sign that these ectoparasites are present. A piece of Shell pest strip may be placed in a milk carton which has had many holes punched in it. This can be hung directly above the tank for a day. Do not use a freshly opened pest strip in this fashion. Instead, let it "age" for at least one day before using it. Ticks are visible and can be removed from the snake using a tweezer. Chemical treatment is generally not necessary. Dispose of the transport bag and container immediately so you will not be tempted to reuse them later. It goes without saying that the utensils we employ for cleaning and feeding in the quarantine container should not be used for any other terrariums. You will probably want to offer some food to your new snake, but give it time first to recover from the trauma of the trip and to get adjusted to its new surroundings. After about twenty-four hours, try feeding your snake, but if it reacts with fright, remove the food animal and wait for two days before you try again.

Terrariums stacked on top of each other and equipped with sliding glass doors are space-saving, easily surveyable, and quick and easy to attend to.

One Snake or a Community of Snakes?

Are Snakes Solitary by Nature?

Snakes do not form communities in the wild. From this fact we can conclude that it is safest to keep them singly in a terrarium, but it is also quite possible to house several snakes together in one space.

Keeping a Community Terrarium

If you do keep several snakes together, there has to be enough space for the snakes to get out of each other's way. There ought to be several retreats offering different temperatures so that optimum conditions are always available. With some snakes, it is preferable not to

31

Basic Rules for Keeping and Caring for Snakes

keep more than one individual of the same species. This is especially true of species that prey on other reptiles in the wild. I myself once suffered an embarrassing loss that I would just as soon keep secret. But since my experience is supposed to help you avoid making the mistakes I made, I will briefly discuss the incident. I had a male Common King Snake *(Lampropeltis getulus holbrooki)* that lived exclusively on mice for two years, and after a long search I found what was obviously a female of the same species. An experienced snake keeper warned me earnestly against housing the two snakes together, but (according to all the literature I could find) it just happened to be the mating season for these snakes, so I decided to take a chance and put the two together. To my delight, after a short time I was able to observe them copulating, and in my mind's eye I already saw myself the proud owner of a batch of baby snakes. I left the two snakes together in the same container. About three weeks later, the female, which was the smaller of the two, could not be found. I searched all the hiding places in the terrarium without success. Then, suddenly, I noticed the unusual posture of the larger snake. It was not coiled up as usual but lay on the heater, forming only one loop. I hardly need to mention that its body was considerably thicker than usual and that over a period of about two weeks, it proceeded to pass its partner, a piece a day and well digested, back into the terrarium.

Feeding also presents some problems in a community terrarium. My six *Elaphe obsoleta quadrivittata*—they were siblings and had lived together from the moment they had hatched—had to be separated at feeding times because these otherwise calm creatures would suddenly burst into frantic activity at the sight of food. Attempts to feed them together by giving each snake its prey as quickly as possible ended in a chaotic mess of tangled bodies tying themselves together in knots, biting each other, and likely to swallow each other in their blind rush for food. I had to resort to the "alcohol treatment," i.e., spraying the snakes' mouths with alcohol to make them let go of each other. If you want to keep several snakes in one terrarium, you should try to do it only with animals that are not overly sensitive, that are used to living in captivity, and that will accept food even when they are removed from their usual surroundings and placed in a feeding box.

How to Move a Snake

Snakes are not animals that like to be handled and petted. It follows that they should be disturbed and touched as little as possible. But sooner or later you will find yourself in a situation when it is necessary to handle your snake, as when you have to move it from one container to another. If we are dealing with a large, aggressive snake, we use a special moving box that is all closed in except for one entry hole. If there is no hurry, we simply wait until the snake on its

Basic Rules for Keeping and Caring for Snakes

own accord chooses this dark space to rest in. We then close off the entry hole and can move the snake without causing it any upset. If we do not have time to wait for the snake to move on its own, we can gently urge it toward the hole with a stick. Small, unaggressive snakes can be picked up with a loose hold around the middle of their bodies and carried this way. We should never grab a snake with a tight hold because that will trigger the reflex action of trying to escape or bite. If you have a phobia about being bitten, you should wear gloves as a precaution.

Be Careful When You Clean the Terrarium

The advice about wearing gloves also applies to the chore of cleaning the terrarium. The novice snake keeper should wear gloves while he is experimenting to find out how close he can get to the snake before it bites. Snakes quickly get used to routine cleaning activities going on around them and will then put up with these disturbances calmly. This is always assuming, of course, that you do not startle them with sudden, hasty movements.

If the Snake Bites

In spite of all precautions, it may happen that the snake bites. This is not very serious if it is simply a quick, defensive bite after which the snake resumes its preattack posture. The instinctive reaction of someone who gets bitten is to jerk back. If the biting and the pulling back happen simultaneously, the result may be unpleasant, especially if the snake is a big constrictor. Its teeth get hooked in the bite wound, causing it to

This is the way to hold small snakes. Take the head between your thumb and forefinger. Prevent the snake from writhing about by pressing its body lightly against your palm with the rest of your fingers.

bite harder, wrap itself around the bitten part of the victim's body, and begin to squeeze. For rare emergencies of this kind you should always have something handy that the snake detests the smell of. In my experience, a few drops of any hard liquor will do the trick. Sprinkle the alcohol over the snake's head, trying to get some on the mucous membranes of the mouth, which the snake has opened for biting. This will send the animal on a speedy retreat. Some snake keepers recommend ammonia or formaldehyde for this purpose, but I do not agree with them because these substances can cause chemical burns.

Note: If you are bitten by a snake, you must go to a doctor immediately to have the wound properly treated.

Breeding Snakes

The collapse of entire ecosystems, the persecution and destruction of snakes, and the irresponsible actions of some profit-hungry reptile dealers who have reportedly stripped whole areas of their snake populations have all contributed to reducing some species of snakes to the point of extinction. We snake enthusiasts are not altogether without blame for this state of affairs, because our demand for snakes, which ultimately determines the supply on the market, has led some dealers to look on reptiles as a mass product with a rewarding profit margin.

Arguments in Favor of Breeding

Anyone who has ever visited a mass supply pet store or a so-called "amateur" snake keeper dealing in reptiles as a profitable sideline, is bound to question the morality of buying even one snake and thus contributing to the trade in reptiles when he sees how these animals are sometimes crowded together by the hundreds in trays stacked one above the other. Some concerned herpetologists refuse to increase their holdings from these sources for this very reason. They either swap with other snake enthusiasts, or they buy from people who need or want to give up their terrariums. This new mentality has, in recent years, caused a number of herpetologists to breed snakes in captivity and cover the demand for pet snakes in this way. Zoos all over the world have successfully raised snakes in captivity and shown that breeding snakes in a terrarium does not have to be a rare event.

Availability of Information

A number of experienced herpetologists have for years been raising several species of snakes. Luckily they do not keep to themselves the conditions that have led to their success, and they often report on their experiences in popular specialized magazines. Any amateur snake keeper, even the novice, should plan from the beginning not only to keep his charges under optimum conditions but also to let them breed.

The conditions necessary for snakes to produce offspring vary a great deal with the different species, and I cannot, within the context of this book, offer specific advice. That is why it is advisable for anyone who intends to keep snakes to join a club of reptile keepers or take out a membership in the American Society of Ichthyologists and Herpetologists (address on page 78). Through these contacts you will be able to find others who are keeping the same kinds of snakes you have and who will be eager to exchange experiences. The members of some breeding associations have recently taken to loaning each other their snakes to increase the probability of producing healthy offspring.

Determining the Sex

Unlike lizards, in which the male can be recognized by various appendages or

Above: Asian Chicken Snake *(Elaphe oxycephala).*
◀ Below: Leopard Snake *(Elaphe situla).*

protuberances, such as a horn on the nose or a comb on the back of the head, snakes generally lack obvious sex characteristics. In some species, a difference in coloration serves as a clue to determining sex; and in most species, one visible difference between males and females is that the base of the tail is broader in the male. This broadening of the tail is caused by two skin pockets, one each for the right and left hemipenis. If you look at several specimens of the same species of snake, you can usually tell the sex of the animals by the proportion between body and tail lengths. Generally, males have a notice-

Behind the head, a snake's skeleton consists of nothing but vertebrae and ribs (200 to 400, in rare cases over 500). Giant snakes still have some vestigial pelvic bones, and anal spurs (arrow) are sometimes visible near the anus.

ably longer tail than females. In adult snakes there is also a difference in overall size; females are usually bigger than males. In the case of pythons, for instance, the female may be as much as six or seven feet (2 m) longer than the male. In addition to these superficial methods of recognizing a snake's sex, I will mention a couple that specialists use. One is to feel with your thumb for the hemipenises on the snake's belly near the base of the tail. But if this is done improperly by an inexperienced person, the snake can be harmed. The newest and most foolproof way of telling a snake's sex is beyond the competence of an amateur. Trained personnel in veterinary medicine take a blood sample from the snake, and by examining its hormonal components they can tell whether it comes from a male or female snake.

Rules of Thumb for Breeding Snakes
The following points should be taken into account if you are considering breeding snakes:
• Keeping a community of snakes can have negative effects. If the snakes are separated and then reunited at mating season, the likelihood that copulation will take place increases.
• Overfed, fat snakes tend to be unenthusiastic about mating.
• Snakes that hibernate in the wild are generally ready to mate when they re-emerge into active life. If you want to breed such snakes, you therefore have to present them with the appropriate hibernating conditions first.

Basic Rules for Keeping and Caring for Snakes

• Often two snakes of the same species that happen to live together in a terrarium do not take to each other. Joining or forming a club with other herpetologists and borrowing or lending sexually mature snakes can circumvent this difficulty and lead to happy results.

• Keeping snakes at the wrong temperature or incorrect level of humidity inhibits their readiness to mate. Compare the conditions that prevail in your terrarium with those that successful breeders of snakes maintain, and make the adjustments that seem indicated. With the technical accessories that are available today, it is possible to simulate practically any climatic conditions in a terrarium.

What to Do in the Case of Unexpected Offspring

Sometimes even snake keepers with no intention of breeding their pets find themselves unexpectedly confronted with a batch of newborn snakes. This can happen if a pregnant snake was inadvertently purchased. In that case, the sight of the baby snakes will come as a complete surprise. The first thing to do is separate the newborn animals from their mother. Plastic aquariums are useful for this purpose. They can easily be equipped with slits or openings for ventilation. Aquarium heating rods with low wattage work best for heating, but they have to be insulated, of course, so that the young snakes do not get burned by them. Usually the baby snakes shed their first skin a few days after birth, and they must not be fed before this happens. If they are healthy, they will then readily accept food—for example, newborn mice. If they refuse to eat for more than a week after shedding, you should consider force-feeding them. If you feel hesitant about attempting this with the tiny creatures, seek the help of someone with more experience in handling snakes.

Measures to Be Taken with Egg-laying Snakes

The preparations necessary for breeding egg-laying snakes are somewhat more involved, since here the mother does not take on the responsibility for incubating and brooding. It is we, the keepers, who have to create the conditions favorable to the proper development of the embryo. The mother usually deposits all her eggs in one clump; that is, the eggs are stuck to each other. Some breeders urge you not to tamper with the eggs but to place them in the incubator just the way you find them in order not to disturb the position of the embryo in relation to the yolk. However, I have noticed no adverse effect from separating the eggs. I usually place the eggs singly and at a small distance from each other on some litter in the incubator. After that, of course, the eggs must not be disturbed. As litter for the eggs I always use a mixture of clean peat moss and sand. This mix has proved successful for maintaining the moisture and warmth necessary for incubation.

Basic Rules for Keeping and Caring for Snakes

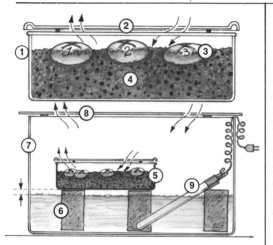

Incubation chamber for breeding snakes. Use a clear plastic container (1) and raise the cover (2) slightly to provide ventilating slits. Lay the marked eggs (3) in a layer of peat moss (4). To maintain the proper temperature in the incubation chamber (5), place it on bricks (6) in a plastic aquarium (7) with a glass cover (8) over it. A thermostatically regulated heater (9) will maintain a constant temperature.

Wintering Over

In the section of this book describing the different snake species, I indicate whether or not hibernation is necessary for the particular snake under discussion.

General Advice
If a snake is ill or emaciated, we should not let it hibernate. Generally speaking, it does no harm to a snake that would hibernate in the wild if it misses this period of rest in the terrarium. But since we want to make every effort to let our animals live normal, natural lives, we should plan on hibernation for those snakes that come from temperate zones or from subtropical areas with large, seasonal fluctuations in temperature. Our reward will be that the snakes will be much more lively during their period of activity. In addition, the rest period during the winter seems to activate the mating instinct, and we probably increase our chances of successfully breeding snakes in captivity by simulating the conditions of a natural winter.

Planning for Winter Rest
If you keep your snakes in a separate room you can winter them over without any elaborate preparations. You simply turn off the heat and the artificial light in the terrarium, as well as the heat in the room, and darken the terrarium. The temperature can occasionally drop down to almost freezing without any harm to snakes like those native to Europe. I am perhaps overly cautious, and I winter my snakes at temperatures between 47° and 56°F (8°–13°C), but to my satisfaction I can say that I have never lost a single snake during hibernation. I never extend the wintering-over period beyond three months. In my opinion, this is long enough, even though some herpetologists recommend up to five months for snakes from North and Central America. If you have no separate terrarium room, you have to house your snakes in a special container that is placed in the cellar or a

Basic Rules for Keeping and Caring for Snakes

refrigerator, but you have to be very careful to make sure that the necessary temperatures prevail. The container should be well-ventilated and filled with a mixture of peat moss and sand with some chunks of bark and moss. Fresh water must always be available, and you should be able to check on the whole setup easily.

The Transition after Hibernation

The return to normal terrarium conditions should not be too abrupt. A gradual increase in the temperature and the amount of light in the terrarium over approximately a week will suit the snake's need to reawaken slowly. Feedings should not be resumed until conditions in the terrarium have returned to normal. Usually only female snakes accept food after hibernating, while males will not start eating again until after the mating period, which, as we have said, follows the hibernation.

Keeping Records

To be able to look back on the development of one's snake, every terrarium buff should write down as much information as possible about the new charge from the day it arrives. Keeping records makes all the more sense if you have several snakes, so you can keep track of when which snake ate last, when it shed last and how the shedding went, and when it last received its vitamins. You should not neglect jotting down notes on temperature and humidity. Having all these records can give you clues to help explain changes in behavior or indicate possible mistakes in environmental conditions in the case of sickness. Since almost all snake keepers collect similar data, it becomes possible to make comparisons and hold discussions of these factors that are informative for you and beneficial for the snakes.

Procuring Food and Feeding the Snakes

Feeding Live Animals

If you give your snakes live animals to eat, you have to stay and watch what happens. A mouse, and even more so a rat, must never be allowed to stay in the terrarium if the snake does not soon respond with interest and kill its prey. Otherwise, the rodent may use its powerful teeth on the snake. Nor should you let fish linger any length of time in the oxygen-poor water of the basin in the terrarium. They would die a slow, painful death. If your water snakes fail to respond to the swimming motions of a fish, catch it and remove it.

Where to Get Prey

The easiest way to get food for your snakes is to buy white mice, hamsters, guinea pigs, or fish at a pet supply store. There is usually no problem about this. Specialty stores for sport fishing carry cheap bait fish, but since these dealers usually carry their fish primarily as a service to fishermen, they are sometimes reluctant to sell them for other purposes.

There are pigeon keepers in most large cities, and they are usually eager to get rid of their excess birds. Get in touch with these people if you need a lot of large food animals for your snakes. Pigeon breeders usually sell even grown birds quite reasonably. If you have a freezer you can also put in a supply of day-old chicks. Thousands of chicks hatch every day on poultry farms, and since only the hens are kept, all the little roosters are killed immediately. It makes sense to get together with other snake keepers to be able to buy in sufficiently large quantities. Most poultry farms do not sell less than one hundred chicks at a time. When you feed frozen chicks, be sure to thaw them long enough and dry the feathers well. Before actually feeding them to the snakes, place them on a warm radiator to warm them through.

If you use live animals, you have to have containers to hold them until feeding time. Pet supply stores sell different models of well-ventilated aquariums for fish and cages for small animals.

How to Raise Food Animals Yourself

Most terrarium keepers with a number of snakes begin to raise their own food animals sooner or later. This requires an extra investment of time, but it has the advantage of significantly lowering the cost of providing food. More important, perhaps, is that you always have food available for your snakes when they get hungry. Raising a laboratory variety of the common house mouse presents no significant problems. The white mouse, an albino variant, is best known and can be bought at any pet store. There are also several colored varieties that can be crossed with each other. If you want to raise mice, it is best to buy a stock of one male and four or five females. It is quite feasible to let mice breed in a regular cage for small mammals, but this method is not the simplest and is quite

41

Procuring Food and Feeding the Snakes

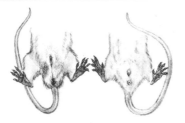

Determining the sex of animals you raise for food for your snakes. The most important detail to note is the distance between the anus and the genitals. Above: Male mouse (left); Female mouse (right). Below: Male hamster (left); Female hamster (right).

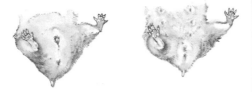

labor intensive. You are better off going to a store specializing in supplies for medical laboratories and getting the kind of containers that have been used for years for the cheap production of laboratory animals. These containers are quite flat, made of plastic, and come equipped with a metal grate, a food tray, and a water dispenser. The mice can be fed dry dog food or pellets made especially for small mammals. The mice thrive best at a temperature of 68° to 74°F (20° to 23°C), and they should be first bred when they are about sixty days old. After about one year, the old parent mice should be replaced by young animals. Before embarking on keeping a mouse colony, you should consider whether you have a suitable room to house the breeding containers. An apartment is not the right place for mice because they may give off an odor even if you clean up after them regularly.

Norwegian rats can be raised just as simply as mice. They, too, come in different colorations. The most popular strain is an albino laboratory rat that is generally raised for experiments in scientific institutions because of its great fertility. The gestation period is only twenty-three days, and these rats often have six litters of up to eight young a year. Rats are kept in the same kind of cages that are used for mice, but they are kept singly rather than in groups of one male with several females. The male rat is placed together with a female only for mating. If you have an aversion toward mice and rats, this does not mean that you have to give up the idea of raising food animals for your snake yourself. The Syrian hamster, or gold hamster, can be bred quite easily in captivity. It produces up to thirteen young per litter. But the females are quite aggressive toward the males and must be kept in separate cages. The two are brought together only when the female is in heat. The young should also be separated from each other once they reach sexual maturity (after about six weeks) because then they may start biting and even killing each other. It hardly pays to raise guinea pigs as food for snakes, because these rodents are not, contrary to popular opinion, very prolific. You cannot count on an annual crop of more than fifteen young, and this is hardly worth the effort involved.

Basic Rules for Keeping and Caring for Snakes

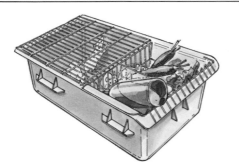

This plastic container for food animals is equipped with a large enough food hopper and water bottle that a terrarium keeper can leave the animals alone for a few days without having to attend to them (available in pet shops).

How Often Should a Snake Be Fed?

This question is difficult to answer. Snakes that are kept under identical conditions, belong to the same species, and are of comparable size may develop very different appetites. Every snake owner has to experiment with his new acquisition to learn what its eating habits and food requirements are. As a basic rule you can assume that young snakes should be offered food about every ten days. Half-grown animals usually have to be fed no more than once every two weeks, while fully grown snakes need food only every three to four weeks.

If Your New Snake Refuses Food

With some snakes, it may be quite a long time before they accept food in their new surroundings. There can be several causes for this.
• The snake may be diurnal or nocturnal and is offered food at the wrong time of day.
• In some species the males fast during the mating season.
• Females often refuse food during the gestation of the young.
• The snake has entered the wintering-over phase of the yearly cycle, and snakes never eat during this phase.
• If the snake is not accustomed to the company of other snakes and is put in with them, this may have an inhibiting effect on it.
• The snake is going through the shedding process, a time when these animals rarely hunt.
• The temperature in the terrarium is less than ideal.
• The size of the food offered is either too large or too small.
• The food offered is not what the snake is used to eating.
The last problem can be a difficult one to solve. A snake that refuses to eat will have to be offered food in all shapes and forms. A snake that refuses to eat live mice may eagerly accept the same animals freshly killed. Some snakes seem to dislike the strong smell of mice. Try giving them young rats or hamsters. To show how varied and unpredictable the food preferences of snakes are, I will tell you about my experience with two Cribos *(Spilotes pullatus),* or Chicken-eaters.

I picked up the two snakes on the same day from the same dealer. Both were of about equal size—55 inches (140 cm)—

43

Basic Rules for Keeping and Caring for Snakes

and were placed together in a terrarium. One of them ate a mouse three days after arrival. Since that did not seem to me enough for a snake of its size, I gave it another mouse a week later, which it devoured without hesitation. From then on this snake ate one mouse per feeding, regardless of whether the meals were at one-week or two-week intervals. It paid not the slightest attention to other prey or to dead mice. The other snake steadfastly refused to eat. It would let a mouse scurry over it, and only when the mouse literally climbed on its head did it respond by rising up vertically, puffing up its throat, and making thrashing motions with its body in typical fright reaction. It ignored dead day-old chicks and live hamsters, and after four weeks of this I

Snakes swallow their prey whole. In most cases, the prey animal is swallowed head first.

seriously began to consider force-feeding it. On the advice of a fellow snake keeper I made one more attempt to induce the snake to eat on its own. I gave it a young rat, and this time I scored success. The snake approached the rat with extreme caution, but after a while it went for it and swallowed it. Now the spell was

broken. From that time on, it would eat up to five prey animals the size of mice at every feeding.

The amounts of food young snakes take can vary just as much. This becomes evident from my experience with two Rat Snakes *(Elaphe obsoleta)* that I raised from the same hatch. In the course of one year, counting from the day of hatching, one of the snakes ate 32 mice, the other 73. As you can see, individual snakes differ in their demand for food, and you have to adjust to their idiosyncrasies to keep them healthy.

Giving Vitamins

It is a good idea to add a multivitamin preparation to every second or third feeding. These products, designed for human consumption, are available in either liquid or capsule form. The latter is relatively easy to use if your snake eats dead day-old chicks. Simply press the capsule inside the chick's beak, and the whole thing will go down. Liquid vitamins are harder to administer since they have a fairly strong odor that may keep the snake from eating. In such a case I usually wait until the food animal is halfway down the snake's gullet before I place a drop of vitamins on it.

Rest Period after Eating

After eating, snakes like to return to their retreats, and they often remain inactive until the whole digestive process is

Basic Rules for Keeping and Caring for Snakes

over. They should be disturbed as little as possible at these times. If they are bothered during this period, or if the temperature in the terrarium is not right, they may regurgitate the food undigested or only partially digested.

Force-Feeding

If snakes go on a hunger strike, this is not necessarily a cause for immediate alarm. But it can happen that these fasts lead to a weakening of the animal. This becomes apparent in clearly visible emaciation: The skin on the snake's sides becomes too big and floppy. Force-feeding becomes necessary at this point. With a small snake you take hold of the head with your thumb and index finger. Hold on to the body with the rest of your fingers and the flat of your hand. With larger snakes, the body is gently pressed against a firm surface with the heel of your hand and the lower arm. Then you pry open the mouth with a flat piece of wood (for baby snakes a wooden match split in half is large enough) that you push in from the side. Now you introduce the food, which you hold with blunt tweezers, into the mouth. At this point the mouth is usually opened wide enough for the strip of wood to fall out, and you can gently push with the tweezers until the food disappears down the esophagus. Frequently the snake will start actively swallowing as soon as it feels the food in its mouth. If this is the case, there is obvi-

ously no longer any need for you to assist the process. Snakes that are being force-fed are usually extremely nervous and have to be handled with great care. Avoid hasty movements and prevent distractions of any kind, because under these conditions snakes tend to regurgitate what they have just eaten. Beef heart, fish, and small, freshly killed rodents are suitable for force-feeding. Food should be given in small amounts, so that the weakened digestive tract is not overtaxed. Force-feeding should be continued until the snake has recovered its strength and starts eating again on its own. Baby snakes generally eat nothing until they have shed their first skin and must therefore never be force-fed. If they still do not eat after shedding, they can be fed some finely ground beef heart mixed with a little egg yolk and with vitamins. For this purpose it is best to use a rubber tube that is attached to a syringe. The tube can be inserted way into the mouth and the food pressed through it. Baby snakes usually start feeding themselves after one such force-feeding.

This is the way to hold the snake and the food animal for force-feeding.

If Your Snake Gets Sick

Experienced snake keepers know that if a snake gets sick after an extended period of living in captivity, this is usually due to improper care or wrong environmental conditions. Of course, it takes years of experience before one is able to objectively assess such errors in care. Someone who has kept snakes for years will generally be able to evaluate his charge's state of health and immediately detect changes in it, even when an equally experienced terrarium enthusiast who is unfamiliar with these particular animals sees nothing wrong.

Preventing Disease

Diseases can generally be prevented if one takes care to recreate in the terrarium, the artificial "segment of environment"—the conditions that prevail in the snake's natural biotope. In doing this, only biological factors such as light, kinds of light rays, warmth, humidity, ventilation, and the availability of hiding and sunbathing places, are of prime significance. Density of population, the size of the container, and the combination of different individuals and species also have to be considered. And it is desirable, of course, that any newcomers you acquire be relatively free of parasites. But we know very little about how far we can safely go in prophylactic measures against "pests" without harming the snake. In nature, many commensal relationships exist in which the "parasite" has no harmful effect as long as the host is healthy. This can remain true of our terrarium snakes as long as no imbalances are caused by incorrect conditions in the terrarium.

Signs of Illness

Changes in Behavior

We soon get familiar with all aspects of behavior of a snake that has adjusted to its surroundings in the terrarium. If we notice a sudden change—for example, a snake may inexplicably refuse food even after we have changed the fare and offered as many alternatives to the usual food as possible—this is usually the first sign that something is amiss. (Exceptions to this are the periods leading up to shedding, pregnancy, mating season, and similar phases during which snakes either reduce or entirely suspend their food intake.)

We should also take note if the snake suddenly stops frequenting its favorite sunning or resting spots. When the animal is so sick that it lets its upper body

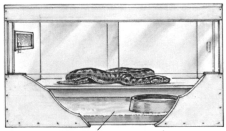

Blotting paper or sand.

Quarantine terrariums for snakes should contain only the bare essentials so that they will be easy to keep clean. The bottom material and the water should be changed frequently and the rest of the terrarium kept spotlessly clean.

droop limply instead of coiling its body, it is high time to do something. At this time physical changes are often evident: the sides of the body look caved in; the vertebrae stick out like a craggy ridge; the eyes are sunken, and the mouth half open. These are all signs of illness at a relatively advanced stage. If a snake does not shed its skin at the appropriate time or if the skin comes off in bits and pieces, this can also be an early symptom of disease.

Visible External Changes

If the skin turns pale, the colors lose their vividness, and the eyes turn cloudy soon after, there is normally no cause for alarm. The snake is simply getting ready to slough off its skin. Many snakes also refuse food at this stage. Other changes of the skin often take the form of a reddening and slight inflammation on the belly side.

Disorders and Injuries of the Skin and Eyes

In most cases, the reddening and slight inflammation of the skin on the belly are the result of improper conditions in the terrarium, such as dirty bottom material, irritating floor covers or paints in new terrariums, and a humidity that is either too high or too low. If the conditions are remedied and a healing salve applied topically, the symptoms will usually disappear. If the condition is allowed to persist, however, it often gives rise, at a

more advanced state, to *mycosis* or *necrosis* underneath the rims of the scales or even on entire scales. Ultimately lesions can develop, that is, injury of considerable portions of the skin. At this stage, sterile conditions must be imposed immediately by disinfecting the container and treating the body parts affected.

Treatment: Apply Betadine solution or an antibiotic paste made of tetracycline. Disinfect the container with Clorox; leave on the terrarium for about one hour, then rinse with clean hot water.

If the snake has difficulties shedding, a bath in lukewarm water with a little manual help usually takes care of the trouble. The difficulties are most likely to occur at the tip of the tail. If this happens, we should aid the shedding process by pulling the rest of the skin off. If this is not done, the tip of the tail, after not shedding its skin several times, may die off.

Inflammation of the eyes can usually be cured by the application of Bacitracin ointment.

In shedding, the snake sloughs off its skin the way we remove a tight-fitting glove. The skin is turned inside out and peeled back.

If Your Snake Gets Sick

Ectoparasites, Mites, and Ticks

Newly imported or freshly caught snakes usually carry ticks or mites. The areas most affected are the rims of the scales, the eyes, and the anal region. If you neglect treating a newcomer to the terrarium against these parasites, the whole snake population may, if you are unlucky, become infected. The best way to get rid of these parasites is to pick them off the snake with pointed tweezers. Of course, you have to proceed with extreme caution. According to Klingelhöffer, most ticks, because of the shedding process of snakes, have to change hosts three times to complete their life cycle. If, in the course of this cycle, a female tick happens to encounter a male, they mate, and the resulting batch of tick eggs can infest the whole terrarium. One species of mite (genus *Ophioptes*), which lives on American snakes, is said to bore holes into the back scales of the snake and establish itself there. The adult females of the medina worm *(phylum Nematoda)* penetrate beneath the scales into the body tissue, causing changes in the skin that indicate their presence. The scales become soft and sticky. Ticks and mites not only weaken their hosts by

The ideal heat source for a quarantine terrarium: embed a low-wattage heater in a lump of heat-conducting filler.

sucking the blood and lymph fluid, but they can also transmit infectious diseases. As a preventive measure against these pests, use the procedure described on page 31. To facilitate the removal of individual ticks, dab them with oil or cod liver oil ointment.

Disorders of Internal Organs

Because it is extremely difficult to recognize internal disorders, they are much harder to treat. If any of the changes in the general state of a snake's health described above are observed, it is essential to keep exact tabs on the animal's food intake and passing of excreta. If the snake vomits or if there is an abnormal pattern of excretion, a sample of the stool must be analyzed by a veterinary laboratory.

Disorders of the Gastrointestinal Tract

Apart from constipation, which can be recognized by feeling the lower region of the snake's belly with your hand, and which is usually caused by an accumulation of hair and teeth from prey in the digestive tract, harmful endoparasites play a major role in disorders of the digestive system. As I mentioned before, ordinarily harmless commensal relationships can get upset by improper living conditions in the terrarium and give rise to an explosion in the parasite population that then becomes pathogenic, that is, encourages disease.

The most frequent disorders of the intestines are *salmonellosis, amoebic dysentery,* and various kinds of *worms.*

Salmonellae can be treated with Chloramphenicol, Neomycin, Chloromycetin, or Paramomicin. Trutnau has administered 50 to 100 mg/kg BW (milligrams per kilogram [2.2 lbs] of body weight) of Chloramphenicol for a period of four to six days without any harm to the snakes or any side effects.

If *amoebic dysentery* goes untreated, it will lead to death within a short time. But it can be successfully combatted with Humatin (Paramomicin) (200 to 500 mg/kg BW up to four times a week).

Trutnau recommends Fenbendazol in doses of 30 to 50 mg/kg BW against intestinal threadworms, roundworms, pinworms, and hookworms and doses of 100 to 200 mg/kg BW of Thibenzol against intestinal eelworms. He also gives Panacur orally in doses of 20 mg/kg BW against intestinal eelworms and threadworms.

The same authority recommends intramuscular injection of 10 to 30 cc of .9% salt solution per kg of body weight against visible symptoms of dehydration following frequent vomiting or diarrhea. As supportive therapy, Boviserin can be given orally through a feeding tube. The proteins are then absorbed directly by the blood.

Colds and Respiratory Infections

Klingelhöffer describes the symptoms of respiratory infections such as pneumonia as follows: the affected snake keeps its mouth open; the lungs are bloated; the upper body is held erect in a vertical position or even bent backwards. The underside of the body shows a deep longitudinal groove, and during exhalation, the throat puffs up like a sack filled with air while the lung empties with a loud whistling sound. Mucous discharges from the nose and mouth are signs of colds that, according to Trutnau, are the consequence of inadequate conditions in the terrarium, such as temperatures that are permanently too high. Bad air is especially harmful. Terramycin, Chloromycetin, Penicillin, and Streptomycin, given orally as well as intromuscularly, have proved effective in treating respiratory disorders. Fifty mg/kg BW of Terramycin together with 10 mg of Penicillin or Streptomycin should be given once a day for five to seven consecutive days.

Infections of the Mouth and Throat Area

Mouth rot *(stomatitis)* is almost always caused by poor hygienic conditions. Bacteria (usually *pseudomonads*) affect the gums first of all. The gums lose their color and begin to exhibit white dots, and later, cheese-like clots that can at first be removed with a swab. Later they expand and cover entire areas, forcing the lips apart and spreading throughout the oral cavity and down the bronchial tubes. The gums recede, teeth can fall out, or the lower jawbone may become exposed. Vitamin therapy with a multivitamin emulsion (given orally) or massive doses of vitamin A and vitamin C. Intramuscular injections of 25 to 50 mg/kg BW of Terramycin-Depot given three times at twenty-four hour intervals brings relief within a few days.

Non-Venomous Snakes and Giant Snakes and How to Keep Them

Individual Species and Hints for Keeping Them

Explanation of the Descriptions

The descriptions of individual species of snakes on the following pages give you concise information about the appearance of a given species, its natural range, the environmental conditions in that range, and the conditions these snakes require in captivity. In some cases you will find several English names for one species. This is because herpetologists, as well as pet dealers, often cannot agree on one official name. You therefore have to rely on the scientific Latin names. You should make the effort to learn these scientific names even if you are a novice snake keeper, because this is the only way you will know for sure just what kind of snake is being offered in a catalogue.

Decorating a snake terrarium with plants is generally not advisable because the animals usually kill the plants by lying on them, and the chapter on setting up a terrarium therefore included no instructions on planting. There are only a few exceptions, mentioned in the following descriptions, where you might consider introducing some exceptionally robust and resistant plants into the terrarium.

Explanations of the symbols next to the English names of the snakes:

- ● = active at dusk and at night
- ○ = active during the day
- ◑ = active day and night
- ◉ = preferably tree-dwelling
- ◒ = preferably ground-dwelling
- ◎ = hibernation recommended

Ringed Snake (photo, page 53) ○ ◒ ◎

Natrix natrix

Length: In Central Europe up to 5 feet (1.5 m); in southwestern Europe up to 6-½ feet (2 m).

The Ringed Snake has a very wide area of distribution. It occurs not only in northern Europe but has been found in northwestern Africa, in Asia, and in southern Siberia as well. The fact that this snake inhabits such a large geographic area indicates that it is extremely adaptable to different environments. Although it is generally considered a water snake, it can and does live in areas far from any accumulations of water. It thrives in wooded areas, moors, and even on land that is in active agricultural use.

An excellent swimmer, this snake moves both in the water and on land with elegant and powerful movements. When it swims, it keeps its head above water. The Ringed Snake lives primarily on amphibians and is no threat to fish populations because it is unable to catch healthy fish. It acts more like an enforcer of health standards by weeding out sluggish fish. It actually eats its prey on land.

The Ringed Snake bites only rarely. When it is bothered, it hisses with its mouth closed. When it is caught, it empties its cloaca, emitting a foul-smelling secretion likely to drive

Some snakes, like the Ringed Snake in this illustration, play dead when threatened with danger. They lie absolutely still with their bodies loosely coiled, their mouths open, and their tongues hanging out.

50

Non-Venomous Snakes and Giant Snakes and How to Keep Them

away the enemy. There is another strategy of defense that has often been observed in grown Ringed Snakes: playing dead. When danger threatens, the snake will curl up in loose coils, open its mouth wide, and let its tongue loll out the side. It will stay in this position for some time.

The mating period of the Ringed Snake begins soon after hibernation in April or May. Depending on the snake's range, eggs are released in June, July, or August, and the young will consequently hatch anywhere from August to early October. One clutch usually consists of 15 to 30 eggs, which are deposited in a compost heap or some other accumulation of decomposing plant matter that generates warmth. Nests used for egg laying by several snakes and often containing several hundred eggs have been found.

Demands in Captivity: The terrarium has to contain a water basin of adequate size as well as hiding places and some absolutely dry spots. Opportunities for climbing should be provided since this snake likes to climb in the wild. The air temperature should be at least 60°F (16°C) at night and no higher than 80°F (26°C) during the day. Additional bottom heat is recommended.

The Ringed Snake is a lively snake that is active during the day, and it gets along well with other members of its species.

Hibernation is not absolutely necessary but advisable. Individual snakes that have hibernated are more lively afterwards than others that have not.

Barred Ringed Snake (photo, page 53)

Natrix natrix helvetica

Length: Up to 80 inches (200 cm). The vernacular name of this snake reflects the markings which clearly distinguish it from the Ringed Snake. This subspecies has dark, barlike markings in the lighter brownish or blue-gray ground color on the sides of the body and tail. Two lines of dark dots run along the back. The Barred Ringed Snake is of stouter build as well as longer than the Ringed Snake. The head is somewhat broader in shape. The range of the Barred Ringed Snake extends from the British Isles to Holland, Belgium, France, the parts of Germany west of the Rhine, Switzerland, some areas of Austria, northern Italy, and northwestern Yugoslavia. This snake prefers regions with moving water and feeds primarily on frogs. The species is egg-laying.

Demands in Captivity: Similar to those of the Ringed Snake. The water basin might be a little larger and have a branch above it for the snake to lie on. Install a small aquarium heater next to the basin, and you will find that this will be one of the snake's favorite spots.

Like its cousin, the Barred Ringed Snake is active during the day. It can be kept together with other snakes of similar needs without problems.

Hibernation: See Ringed Snake, page 53.

Striped Ringed Snake

Natrix natrix persa

Length: Variable.

This is an extremely interesting subspecies in terms of its coloration and markings. Because of the great variation in markings, it is difficult to accurately determine the species of this snake in the different areas in which it occurs. It may even happen that snakes from the same hatch look different—some may be striped while others are spotted. The area of distribution includes Turkey, Greece, Bulgaria, Albania, and Yugoslavia. Some com-

Non-Venomous Snakes and Giant Snakes and How to Keep Them

pletely black individuals have been found, especially in isolated areas such as the Greek islands. It is just as impossible to say anything definite about the length of this snake as it is to give an accurate description of its markings. The length, too, varies. There are populations of small snakes, and there are others where large size is the rule.

Demands in Captivity: Striped Ringed Snakes like to climb and are active during the day, but they are generally somewhat shyer than other Ringed Snakes. It is fairly easy to get them to accept non-live food such as strips of fish, and they therefore present few problems to their owners.

Like other Ringed Snakes, this subspecies can be kept in a community terrarium.

Hibernation: See Ringed Snake, page 53.

Viperine Snake (photo, page 53) ○ ◒ ◉

Natrix maura

Length: Rarely over 40 inches (100 cm).

This water snake, probably the prettiest of the European species, ranges from southwestern Switzerland, northwestern Italy, southern France, and some islands of the Mediterranean to the Iberian peninsula and northwestern Africa.

The head is clearly marked off from the neck, and the zigzag pattern of the markings on the back gives further rise to the impression that this is a venomous snake. The ground color of the body is gray-brown, olive green, or yellow-brown, and the underside is a speckled yellowish brown. Klingelhöffer reports that 150 to 200 snakes may congregate at the mating season in spring (March to April). In June or July, each female will deposit 4 to 20 eggs in loose soil,

under flat rocks, or in decayed plant material. The young, measuring 6 to 8 inches (15–20 cm), hatch in August or early September. According to Klingelhöffer, Viperine Snakes like clear water and are sometimes found by the sea as well. I had the opportunity of catching and observing several of these snakes in southern Spain. They liked to play around on the surface of the water, sunned themselves on algae islands in shallow waters, and would dive off and burrow into the bottom at the slightest disturbance. A number of these snakes would also appear at a large artificial basin and spend the whole year from the mating period to hibernation there. These snakes are dependent on plenty of moisture or open areas of water.

Demands in Captivity: The Viperine Snake has no great need to climb. Instead it likes to lie on flat rocks or algae growth and sun itself. These diurnal snakes need temperatures between 72° and 92°F (22°–33°C) and sunlight or ultraviolet light for at least part of the day. Frogs, fish, and earthworms can be offered for food.

The terrarium should be set up as an aqua-terrarium with a climbing branch rising out of the water basin and several platforms for resting. Moss, sand, and forest soil make good bottom material

Viperine Snakes have been successfully

Above: Viperine Snake *(Natrix maura)* (left) and ▷ King Snake *(Lampropeltis getulus)* (right).
Center: Indigo Snake *(Drymarchon corais)* (left) and Cribo or Chicken Eater *(Spilotes pullatus)* (right).
Below: Black Chicken Snake, baby snake just hatched from egg *(Elaphe obsoleta)* (left) and Barred Ringed Snake *(Natrix natrix helvetica)* (right).

bred in captivity. At an incubation temperature of 77° to 86°F (25°–30°C), the young hatch after about 40 to 45 days.

Hibernating conditions can be set up from November to May. For this it is a good idea to lower the nighttime temperature by 9° to 15°F (5°–8°C).

Keelback Snake

Natrix piscator

Length: Up to 4 feet (1.2 m).

This snake comes from southern Asia and Malaysia and is always found near water. The head of this slender snake is set off from the neck only slightly, and the tail is relatively long. The ground color of the back is yellowish to reddish brown with, usually, five parallel rows of spots running from head to tail. The belly side is cream-colored. Two narrow black lines run from below and behind the eyes to the corners of the mouth.

If the Keelback Snake feels threatened, it raises its upper body, flattened and cobra-like, and is quick to bite. Frogs bitten by this snake have shown symptoms of poisoning. Keelback Snakes can be given fish and sometimes mice for food.

Demands in Captivity: A large part of the terrarium should be taken up with a water basin. The "land area" can consist of a mixture of sand, peat moss, and forest soil. Hollow tree stumps or flat rocks can offer hideaways. Air temperature should range from 75° to 86°F (24°–30°C) with several hours of direct sunlight or ultraviolet radiation. Localized bottom heat is advisable.

The Keelback Snake has also been raised in captivity. This snake lays 8 to 87 eggs, which hatch after an incubation period just short of three months at 77° to 86°F (25°–30°C).

Hibernation: A rest period in the winter or summer, depending on the snake's place of origin, is recommended.

Common Water Snake

Natrix sipedon

Length: Up to 53 inches (1.35 m).

The Common Water Snake is the most widely distributed North American snake of the *Natrix* genus, occurring from southern Canada to the Carolinas and western Colorado. In body shape it very closely resembles the Ringed Snake. One sixth of the overall length is taken up by the tail. The coloration of the Common Water Snake varies from gray to reddish brown on the back. The belly is white with red and black marks. The upper back and the neck have dark crossbands which get wider lower down on the flanks. The pupils of the eyes are round, as in all members of the *Natrix* genus. Like its European counterpart, it bites and secretes a foul-smelling substance when it feels attacked or annoyed. Its natural habitat is also comparable to that of the European version. It lives in swamps and wet areas near bodies of water.

Demands in Captivity: Ideally, the terrarium should be set up as an aqua-terrarium of generous proportions with plenty of branches and bushes rising out of the water. Active during the day, this snake should have daytime temperatures of 68° to 82°F (20°–28°C). At night the temperature should drop to about 60° to 65°F (16°–18°C). Occasional or regular exposure to direct sunlight or ultraviolet radiation is necessary for the snake's well-being.

This snake has been successfully bred in captivity several times. Up to 46 young are born at a time. Fish and amphibians provide food.

Non-Venomous Snakes and Giant Snakes and How to Keep Them

Common Garter Snake (photo on back cover) ○ ◑ ◉

Thamnophis sirtalis

Length: Up to 50 inches (1.25 m).

This snake is very popular and is often kept in terrariums. It is easy to take care of and if properly looked after, it is likely to reproduce in captivity.

One of the most extensive genera of North American snakes, the garter snakes occur in 23 species and many subspecies from southern Canada throughout the United States and down to Mexico. The most abundant and most widely distributed species is the *Thamnophis sirtalis,* which ranges from southern Canada through the United States. In appearance the small and slender Common Garter Snake resembles the European Ringed Snake. The head is only slightly set off from the body, and the tail is relatively long. The scales are keeled, and the top of the head is black or dark brown. The body's ground color varies considerably, and generally a lighter line runs down along the spine with a parallel line on either side. In some individuals the side lines are not present. Others have a pretty pattern of spots on the flanks. Common Garter Snakes are found mostly in moist areas.

Demands in Captivity: The terrarium should include a very large water basin or be set up as an aqua-terrarium (see Green Snake, page **58)**. The temperature should range between 60° and 82°F (20°–28°C). A drop in temperature at night and direct sunlight or ultraviolet radiation during the day are essential.

After getting used to their new setup, these snakes will take food (earthworms, fish, strips of fish, slugs, and tadpoles) from the hand of the keeper.

Hibernation: 2 to 3 months.

Smooth Snake   ○ ◑ ◉

Coronella austriaca

Length: Rarely over 28 inches (70 cm).

The Smooth Snake ranges across almost all of the northern Europe and as far as Asia Minor. It is found only rarely in terrariums because it feeds on lizards, which are protected in many countries. Characteristic for this species is the small, flat, oval head with round pupils and a dark brown stripe running from the nostrils across the eyes to the corners of the mouth. Two to four rows of dark spots stand out from the ground color of the back, which is brown in males and gray to brownish gray in females. The back of the head carries a horseshoe-shaped mark that opens toward the front. Smooth Snakes live in flat as well as in hilly terrain, and are often found on dry slopes and in hedgerows. They kill their prey by wrapping their bodies around it before eating it. Apart from lizards (including blindworms), they eat young snakes, mice, song birds, lizard eggs, earthworms, crickets, grasshoppers, and slugs.

Demands in Captivity: The terrarium can incorporate local woods plants and be equipped with loose, sandy soil, a water basin, and something to climb on. The terrarium should be kept at about 68° to 80°F (20°–27°C), with some exposure to direct sunlight. A drop in temperature at night is recommended. You should not try to do without localized bottom heat. The snakes often spend hours in these hot spots to warm themselves.

The live-bearing Smooth Snake gives birth in September to 2 to 15 young measuring about 6 inches (15 cm).

Hibernation is absolutely essential.

Non-Venomous Snakes and Giant Snakes and How to Keep Them

Common King Snake (photo, page 53) ○◒◉

Lampropeltis getulus

Length: 5 to 6 feet (1.5–1.8 m).

King Snakes are found from southern Oregon to California and Mexico and in the eastern United States. The head is hardly set off from the neck at all, and the large eyes with their round pupils are another distinguishing feature. The ground color is black with narrow white-to-yellowish crossbands that form a decorative chainlike pattern on the back and sides. This snake's natural habitat consists of flat land below 2400 feet (800 m) of altitude, including pine woods, sandy hills, bushy slopes, and tree growths along water.

Demands in Captivity: The terrarium should have sand on the bottom with some pieces of bark and rocks to hide under. A bowl for drinking water must also be provided. The King Snake is an undemanding pet that, once it is settled in, will accept food from its keeper's hand. Daytime temperatures should range between 75° and 86°F (24°–30°C) with a night-time drop to 68°F (20°C). Artificial lighting should be provided all day. The snake can be fed small mammals, birds, and eggs. It has been bred successfully in captivity. Mating takes place after hibernation, and 3 to 30 longish eggs are deposited sometime between June and August. The baby snakes, measuring about 10 to 12 inches (25–30 cm), hatch after 60 to 120 days. The first skin is shed after about 2 weeks, and then the young snakes can be fed baby mice.

Hibernation: Several months of hibernation at about 50°F (10°C) are advisable.

Milk Snake

Lampropeltis triangulum

Length: This brightly colored snake is native to the United States and Central America. It is slender, has a small head that is hardly set off from the body, and has distinct markings. A white, V-shaped mark on the neck, edged in black, stands out against the darker color of the head. A dark line connects the eyes and continues across the temples to the corners of the mouth. Several subspecies have red, black, and yellow (or sometimes white) crossbands. The Milk Snake has dark, black-rimmed saddle marks. The abdomen has black spots or dark crossbands. The habitat of the various subspecies varies considerably from dry to wet conditions.

Demands in Captivity: These snakes are best kept in terrariums of moderate size with loose bottom material composed of sand and peat moss and a few large rocks or pieces of bark that offer opportunities to hide. The temperature should range from 77° to 86°F (25°–30°C). These snakes, which are active at dusk and at night, can be fed young mice. They should always be kept singly because they are sometimes cannibalistic.

Successful breeding of these snakes has been accomplished a number of times. The snakes mate after hibernation; 6 to 24 eggs are laid sometime in July or August, and after an incubation period of about two months at 75° to 80°F (24°–28°C), the young hatch.

Hibernation: Winter rest of several months is recommended.

Non-Venomous Snakes and Giant Snakes and How to Keep Them

Green Snake (photo, page 17) ○ ◉ ◎

Opheodrys aestivus, Opheodrys vernalis

Length: Can exceed 40 inches (100 cm).

Both the Rough-scaled *(O. aestivus)* and the Smooth Green Snake *(O. vernalis)* feed largely on insect prey and are therefore interesting subjects for study in a terrarium.

The Rough-scaled Green Snake is found in the southern U.S. and Mexico, while the Smooth Green Snake ranges from southern Canada to Texas, where it lives in flat as well as hilly terrain and occurs even at altitudes of 10,000 feet (3,000 m) and more. But it does not do well living in an aquarium. Its rough-scaled cousin seems to thrive better under these conditions.

The head of this grass-green, slender snake is somewhat set off from the neck. This snake (which, when seen from above, blends in completely with green foliage) has an egg-shell-colored to yellowish belly. Mostly arboreal in its habits, the snake prefers low trees, bushes, and grass, and it is most often found in thick shore vegetation, but it can also be aquatic and spend much of its time in water.

Demands in Captivity: The terrarium should include a large water basin or be set up as an aqua-terrarium with many forked branches. A mixture of sandy forest soil and peat moss makes a good bottom material. Bottom heating is unnecessary, but the air temperature should vary within the terrarium from 77° to 86°F (25°–30°C). At night the temperature should drop, but no more than 9°F (5°C). A trademark of this snake is that, instead of flicking its tongue, it sticks it out straight and motionless. Direct sunlight does not seem to be required, but artificial lighting for 12 to 14 hours a day is advisable.

The Green Snake lives on small reptiles and insects, such as spiders, beetles, grasshoppers, caterpillars, scorpions, and centipedes. In June or July it lays 3 to 11 eggs from which the five-inch-long young emerge in August or September.

Hibernation: It is advisable to let Green Snakes hibernate for about four months.

Balkan Racer (photo, page 17) ○ ◒ ◎

Coluber gemonensis

Length: Up to about 40 inches (100 cm).

The range of the Balkan Racer extends from Istria, along the Adriatic coast of the Balkans to the Peloponnesus, Crete, and some other Greek islands. The snake's back is gray-brown with irregular dark crossbars and white dots, markings which on the lower body fade into indistinct dark bands. The abdomen is yellow without markings.

C. gemonensis has a general reputation of being a highly aggressive snake that bites at the slightest provocation and whose violent temper hardly subsides even after years of captivity. Furthermore, many herpetologists are convinced that this snake is not suited for terrarium life because it can seriously injure its snout in trying to escape through an improperly installed vent.

Demands in Captivity: This diurnally active snake needs air temperatures of 72° to 82°F (22°–28°C) with some areas kept even warmer by bottom heating. The dry terrarium should be very generous in size, have gravel on the bottom, and be equipped with some sturdy and twisted branches and a large water basin. Lowering the temperature a few degrees at night is recommended.

Small birds, mice, grasshoppers, butterflies, and moths can be offered as food.

Hibernation: A brief hibernating period is recommended.

Non-Venomous Snakes and Giant Snakes and How to Keep Them

European Whip Snake ○ ◑ ◉

Coluber jugularis caspius

Length: Up to 10 feet (3 m).

C. *jugularis caspius* is the largest European snake. The other three subspecies of the European Whip Snake rarely get longer than about 6 feet (1.8 m). *C. jugularis caspius* occurs in southeastern Europe and Western Asia, where it lives on the steppes and on bushy slopes, finding refuge in rock crevices and in thick shrubbery. This snake moves extremely fast and "whips" along the ground. If pursued, it may dart into the burrow of a small mammal and disappear. If it is cornered, it will bite wildly, causing serious wounds, and Klingelhöffer reports that it will even attack humans and sometimes horses whose lips it may hang onto with its teeth.

Characteristic of this powerful snake is its longish head, slightly set off from the neck, and its long tail. The coloration varies from olive gray to brown and black. The keelless scales have yellow lines running down the middle that form continuous lines down the body. The top of the head has dark patches, and the belly can be yellowish brown, reddish, or black.

This snake can be recommended for keeping in captivity only with serious reservations, because its violent nature hardly changes even after years of life in a terrarium.

Demands in Captivity: The terrarium has to be very large and offer several places of refuge. The bottom should be covered with a hard soil of sand, clay, and stones. Opportunities for climbing should be offered in the form of tree limbs with lots of branches, and a solidly anchored water basin is essential. Direct sunlight or an ultraviolet lamp and temperatures between 77° and 86°F (25°–30°C) are important for the snake's well-being. The Whip Snake can be cannibalistic and should therefore be kept singly. Chicks, rats, and mice can be offered as food.

Hibernation: This snake requires several months of hibernation.

Dark Green Racer ○ ◑ ◉

Coluber viridiflavus

Length: Up to 6 feet (1.8 m).

This snake occurs in northeastern Spain, in France, in northwestern Yugoslavia, in Italy, and on some Italian islands. It is slender, has a long tail, and the longish head is only slightly set off from the neck. The ground color of the back is blackish green, and yellowish green speckling forms cross-bands on the upper half of the body and changes into parallel longitudinal stripes toward the tail. The abdomen is yellowish gray to olive green with dark patches toward the sides. The snake prefers dry, rocky terrain with shrubbery. It moves with extreme speed, is hard to catch, and is quick to bite.

C. *viridiflavus* is active during the day and hunts along the ground and among bushes for birds, lizards, small mammals, reptiles— including other snakes—amphibians, grasshoppers, beetles, and even snails. Cases of cannibalism have been reported, so that it is safer to keep this snake singly in a terrarium.

Demands in Captivity: A terrarium of generous proportions should include a sandy and rocky bottom, opportunities for hiding, solid branches for climbing, and a water basin.

Up to now no successful breeding of the Dark Green Racer in captivity has been reported, and the information on the biology of reproduction given here is intended to assist future efforts in this direction. Mating

Non-Venomous Snakes and Giant Snakes and How to Keep Them

takes place in April or May, and about 8 to 15 eggs are deposited any time from the end of June to early September. The eggs hatch after about 6 to 8 weeks, and the young measure about 10 inches (25 cm).

Horseshoe Racer (photo, page 17)

Coluber hippocrepis

Length: Up to 5 feet (1.5 m); rarely up to 6-½ feet (2 m).

This species ranges from the Iberian Peninsula to northeastern Africa and is found on Pantellaria. The tail takes up about a fifth of the length of this slender, almost black snake. A strikingly handsome pattern is formed on the back by lighter, laterally oriented, rhombic blotches. The head has a marking in the shape of a horseshoe. The belly is yellowish to orange and has black patches toward the tail.

The Horseshoe Racer prefers dry, rocky areas with bushy growth. This mostly ground-dwelling snake likes to spend much of its time in the burrows of rodents or hidden underneath rocks. It is active both during the day and at night and hunts small mammals, birds, and lizards. In captivity, it will accept prey both alive and dead.

Demands in Captivity: The Horseshoe Racer is easy to keep in a terrarium. The temperature should be between 70° and 86°F (22°–30°C), and the snakes like to frequent a spot that is warmed by a bottom heater. Mating period is in April or May, and 5 to 10 eggs are produced in the summer. The young emerge between July and September, depending on the date of the egg laying.

The dry terrarium should have a floor of sand and clay, and it should be equipped with a small water basin and hiding places

that can be checked on. The snakes should be exposed to sunlight or ultraviolet light every day.

Hibernation: Several months of hibernation are advisable.

Aesculapian Snake (photo on inside back cover)

Elaphe longissima

Length: Up to 6-½ feet (2 m).

This snake, whose name derives from the Greek god of healing, Aesculapius, is unfortunately now quite rare. Its range extends from northeastern Spain through central and southern Europe to Asia Minor and central Asia. The slender snake has smooth scales and a longish head hardly set off at all from the neck. The tail takes up about one-third of the animal's length. The shiny coloration of the back can vary from yellowish brown to brown and black. Most of the dorsal scales have white streaking on the upper and lower edges. Young snakes have a yellow mark on the back of the head and are therefore often mistaken for the Ringed Snake. The belly is cream-colored. The natural habitat of the Aesculapian Snake is a dry, sandy to rocky terrain with bushy growth. The snake is also found in deciduous woods and old, dilapidated stone walls.

Demands in Captivity: This snake likes to live in an uncramped dry terrarium that has climbing branches, tree stumps, and flat rocks, as well as a good sized water basin. The temperature should vary in the terrarium from 68° to 86°F (20°–30°C) and cool down at night by several degrees. Localized bottom heat is recommended, as is periodic exposure to ultraviolet light or natural sunlight. The breeding of Aesculapian Snakes in captivity

Non-Venomous Snakes and Giant Snakes and How to Keep Them

has been successfully accomplished a number of times. The females deposit 5 to 6 (sometimes up to 18) eggs from which the 7- to 8-inch long baby snakes hatch after about 50 to 60 days of incubation. Small rodents, especially mice, can be offered as food.

Hibernation: A hibernation period of several months is recommended.

Four-lined Rat Snake

Elaphe quatuorlineata

Length: up to 100 inches (2.5 m).

The Four-lined Rat Snake, which can grow to almost 4 inches (9–10 cm) in diameter, makes a pleasant and placid, almost phlegmatic terrarium inhabitant. The range of this snake reaches from Italy to Yugoslavia and Greece. In the Balkans and southern Russia, it is represented by the subspecies *E. quatuorlineata sauromates,* which lives exclusively in the steppes. The body of this species is powerful, and the head only lightly set off from the neck. The ground color of the back is light or dark brown with four decorative black stripes or rows of dark spots running along the body and growing indistinct toward the tail. A dark streak extends from the eyes to the corners of the mouth. The markings of young snakes are very different from those of older individuals. The young are light gray with black markings on the head and longitudinal rows of large dark blotches. The change to adult marking is not completed until the snake is four years old.

The Four-lined Rat Snake lives in varied habitats ranging from rocky dry slopes with scrub growth to marshy shore land. It lives in the same area all its life and is active only on overcast days.

In Italy, Four-lined Rat Snakes are captured for religious festivals and carried around at famous snake processions.

Like the *Dasypeltis scabra* of Africa, the Four-lined Rat Snake has developed a special method for breaking bird eggs when swallowing them. The lower protuberances of some vertebrae are so positioned that they point forward at an angle in such a way that the shell of an egg passing down the gullet will open and be crushed, releasing its contents to the stomach.

Klingelhöffer has stilled the mammoth appetites of these snakes with guinea pigs, moles, rats, and newborn cats and dogs. Mice, sparrows, and reptiles were also included in the fare.

Mating can take place from the spring to the fall. Six to 16 eggs are deposited, in July or August, and in September or October the young snakes hatch, measuring about 9 inches (23 cm).

Demands in Captivity: The bottom of the terrarium should be covered with a mixture of sand and peat moss, on which strips of decorative cork or flagstones are placed to provide hiding places. A largish water basin is also needed. Periodic exposure to ultraviolet light or sunlight is also recommended at a daytime terrarium temperature of 77° to 86°F (25°–30°C).

Hibernation: These snakes should be allowed to hibernate for several months.

Ladder Snake (photo, page 17) ● ◒ ◉

Elaphe scalaris

Length: Five feet (1.5 m) at most.

The Ladder Snake is found in southern France, on Minorca, and on the Iberian peninsula. The impression of stoutness is reinforced by the almost straight line from body to head. As in the case of the Four-lined Rat Snake, the coloration varies with age. Grown individuals exhibit a ladderlike pattern made up of two longitudinal stripes against a brownish background. The abdomen is a uniform yellowish color. Young snakes are brownish yellow with regular crosswise patches. In the wild, *E. scalaris* prefer a dry habitat with lots of hot sunshine in which they like to bask, lying on hillside gravel or rock piles. In the spring they are usually active in the daytime, whereas in the summer they come alive at dusk or during the night. Their preferred prey are mice, but they will also catch lizards and birds. The young eat grasshoppers as well.

Demands in Captivity: When this snake is new to the terrarium it is wild and agitated, biting whenever it can. Once it gets used to its surroundings, it calms down, gets somewhat tamer, and likes to eat. Mating takes place in May and June; in July or August, 5 to 24 eggs are deposited and hatch after 5 to 12 weeks.

This snake should be kept in a dry terrarium at daytime temperatures of 79° to 86°F (26°–30°C) with a drop of temperature during the night.

The terrarium can be set up in similar fashion to that for a Four-lined Rat Snake (see page 61).

Hibernation: These snakes need to hibernate for several months.

Leopard Snake (photo, page 36)

Elaphe situla ◑ ⬤ ◉

Length: Up to 40 inches (100 cm).

This snake is generally considered the handsomest and most colorful of the Euro-pean snakes, and it is a favorite of terrarium buffs, especially since it seems possible to breed it in captivity.

The Leopard Snake is found in southern Italy, on Sicily and Malta, the Balkan peninsula, the northern Sporades, the Cyclades, Crete, in the Caucasus, and on the Crimean peninsula.

The head of this slightly built snake is relatively small and is set off from the neck. The tail takes up about one-sixth of the overall length. The color of the back is light yellow, reddish, or gray and is interspersed with reddish, black-rimmed patches. Each side has a row of brown spots that are not connected to the dorsal patches. The stomach is covered with dark speckles.

Demands in Captivity: Initially, the care of Leopard Snakes in captivity seems difficult and demanding, but after a period of adjustment to the new home and under optimal terrarium conditions, these snakes may be kept successfully and may even produce offspring. A dry terrarium should offer a sandy bottom, opportunities for hiding, climbing branches, and a water basin. Leopard Snakes are active during the day and at dusk and are comfortable at temperatures between 72° to 83°F (22°–28°C). A nightly drop in temperature by a few degrees is necessary, and the snake should have a chance to bask in natural or artificial sunlight.

The mating season is from May to June; in July or August, 2 to 5 relatively large eggs are deposited, from which the young (up to 14 inches long) will hatch after 60 to 70 days of incubating at 76° to 83°F (24°–28°C). Mice are offered as food.

Hibernation: These snakes need several months of hibernation.

Above: Javelin Sand Boa *(Eryx jaculus)* (left) and
Garden Tree Boa *(Corallus enydris)* (right).
Center: Indian Python *(Python molurus)* (left) and
Ball Python *(Python regius)* (right).
Below: Black-headed Python *(Aspidites
melanocephalus)* (left) and Blood Python *(Python
curtus)* (right).

Corn Snake (photos, page 17 and on back cover) ◑ ◒ ◉

Elaphe guttata

Length: Can exceed 6 feet (1.8 m).

This attractive snake with its stunningly beautiful markings is found in the southern United States and in northeastern Mexico. The ground color ranges from rust brown to brick red and orange, and the back and sides have regular red brown markings. There is a V-shaped mark on the nape of the neck and a band running from the eyes to the corners of the mouth. The abdomen has slate blue patches, and the scales are black-keeled. The snake is of slender build with a small head well set off. The pupils are round. Corn Snakes live not only in corn fields but also in open, sunlit pine woods, abandoned plantations, along road sides, and in old walls. Their hunting territory extends from underground burrows of small mammals to the tops of trees, and they go after birds, mice, and young rats. In the spring they are active during daytime, whereas in the summer they do not emerge from their hiding places until dusk.

Demands in Captivity: The Corn Snake is a great favorite among terrarium buffs because it survives well in captivity and can be bred quite easily. It is best to use a mixture of sand and peat moss for the bottom. The terrarium should have a water basin, rocks or pieces of bark to hide under, and a bottom heater. The temperature should range from 72° to 82°F (22°–28°C) with some periods of natural or artificial sunlight and a drop of temperature at night down to 65°F (18°C). A spring mating will usually produce 12 to 14 eggs, stuck together in a clutch, sometime between May and July, and the young snakes hatch a good two months later, measuring 9 to 9-½ inches (22–24 cm). After shedding their first skins they will eat baby mice and can be raised without difficulties.

Hibernation: If you hope for offspring from your snakes, they should be allowed to hibernate at 41° to 54°F (5°–12°C).

Rat Snake (photo, page 54) ◑ ◒ ◉

Elaphe obsoleta

Length: Over 8 feet (2.5 m).

This snake, which is usually black, ranges from northeastern Canada across the United States to Mexico. The Rat Snake is powerfully built with a long, narrow head that is almost continuous with the body. The scales on the upper side of the body have some white edges, and the skin between the scales often looks red. The underside of the body is whitish. The snake is found in dry as well as moist habitats, in plains as well as in mountains. An excellent climber, it often hides way up in trees where it lies in wait for birds. Other elements of its diet are small mammals, amphibians, and eggs.

Demands in Captivity: Choose a terrarium of large proportions with a built-in water basin for this snake, equip it with climbing branches, and use sand as bottom material. Rat Snakes thrive at 72° to 82°F (22°–28°C) with a nightly drop down to 65°F (18°C). Under these conditions they often live for many years in captivity and sometimes produce offspring. Mating takes place after hibernation, and 6 to 44 eggs are deposited in June or July. After an incubation of 2 to 3 months at 77° to 81°F (25°–27°C) the young snakes, measuring 10 to 15½ inches (25–39 cm), hatch. They accept food readily after shedding their first skin.

Hibernation: Hibernation is advisable.

Non-Venomous Snakes and Giant Snakes and How to Keep Them

Asian Chicken Snake (photos on front cover and on page 36)   ○ ◉

Elaphe oxycephala

Length: Up to 7½ feet (2.3 m).

The distribution of this snake reaches from the eastern Himalayas to Thailand, Cambodia, South Vietnam, Burma, Malaysia, the Sunda islands, and the Philippines. This agile, shiny snake of a magnificent green color glides through its habitat of bushy shores in quick motions. It is most often found in wet lowlands and thickly wooded river valleys. With its green coloration it blends in perfectly with the foliage of trees and will bite any intruder. For a long time it was considered a poor bet for terrarium use because it seemed fussy and did not survive very long. But in the meantime it has been bred in captivity. Apart from its spectacular color, the characteristic features of this snake are its long, pointed head and its round pupils. The body is flattened on the sides, and a black line runs from the snout across the eyes to the neck. The tail is yellowish brown and the abdomen yellowish.

Demands in Captivity: The large terrarium should have sturdy tree limbs with lots of branches. Use clean, washed sand for the bottom. The daytime temperature should be between 81° and 90°F (27°–32°C) with artificial lighting all day long. At night the temperature should drop, but not below 72°F (22°C). It is important to keep the humidity even at 80 to 100%. Mice and chicks can be offered as food. As far as breeding is concerned, an incubation temperature of about 82° to 83°F (28°C) is required. The young snakes, measuring about 18 inches (45 cm) will hatch after 14 to 17 weeks.

Indigo Snake (photo, page 53)   ○ ◖

Drymarchon corais

Length: Up to 9 feet (2.7 m).

The Indigo Snake, which ranges from the southeastern U.S. down to Argentina, is considered an ideal terrarium snake that becomes tame quickly. Its natural habitat consists of pine and oak forests or sandy hills with palm trees. Its other name, Gopher Snake, derives from its habit of frequenting areas inhabited by gopher tortoises *(Gopherus polyphemus)* and disappearing into their burrows when frightened. The Indigo Snake's head is somewhat set off from the neck, and the powerful body is somewhat flattened on the sides. The color of the snake varies, depending on its place of origin, from a metallic dark blue to brown. Some individuals are reddish brown to orange at the neck and lower jaw.

Demands in Captivity: This diurnally active, sun-loving snake needs an air temperature of 77° to 79°F (25°–26°C) and a bottom temperature of up to 86°F (30°C) and more. A nightly drop to 68° to 72°F (20°–22°C) is advisable. A terrarium of generous proportions with a relatively large water basin is essential. The bottom can consist of a mixture of sand and peat moss. Hiding places have to be provided.

Initial threatening behavior, such as hissing accompanied by puffing up the throat, flattening the head, and vibrating the tail, will disappear after a short period of acclimatization. The diet of this snake consists of chicks, birds, small mammals, fish, and eggs. Shedding occurs at short intervals, usually every 4 to 6 weeks. Successful breeding in captivity has been reported several times. The snakes mate in November, and the eggs hatch after 12 to 14 weeks.

Hibernation: These snakes can be allowed to hibernate briefly at 65° to 68°F (18°–20°C).

Non-Venomous Snakes and Giant Snakes and How to Keep Them

Cribo or **Chicken Eater** (photo, page 53) ○ ◉

Spilotes pullatus

Length: About 10 feet (3 m); sometimes as much as 13 feet (4 m).

The range of the Chicken Eater, one of the biggest serpents of this type in South America, extends from southern Mexico to Brazil and Argentina, where the snake lives in tropical rain forests or in bushy or wooded areas near water. The body of this brightly colored snake is flattened on the sides to produce a roughly triangular shape when seen in cross section. Slender in build, the snake has a relatively long tail and a head that is only slightly set off from the body. The ground color is lemon yellow against which dark diagonal bands stand out boldly. The belly is orange to yellow, occasionally with black spots.

Active during the day, the Chicken Eater hunts for song birds, small mammals, lizards, frogs, and snakes on the ground as well as in tree tops.

Demands in Captivity: In the terrarium, this snake can be fed mice, chicks, and rats. One Chicken Eater even consumed Common Vipers in captivity, killing them first by constriction. This behavior is characteristic of the species. The snake strikes its prey with wide open mouth and coils its body around it, either squeezing it to death or crushing it against the ground. This easily angered snake, which rarely gets tame in captivity, is very aggressive and bites at the slightest provocation. When it is angry it puffs out its neck vertically, not laterally as the cobra does, and flips its tail, producing a rattling sound similar to that of a rattlesnake.

A terrarium for this large snake has to be of generous proportions and equipped with a large water basin and sturdy climbing branches. The bottom can be covered with a mixture of sand and gravel. The temperature has to be around 75° to 86°F (24°–30°C) during the day and slightly lower at night. Periodic exposure to sunshine or ultraviolet light is recommended.

So far no births in captivity have been reported.

Indian Rat Snake or **Dhaman** ◑ ◒ ◉

Ptyas mucosus

Length: Up to 12 feet (3.6 m).

This species is found from the USSR throughout Central Asia to southern and southeastern Asia, inhabiting lowlands as well as hilly terrain without dense vegetation. This fiery and quite aggressive snake chases after prey along the ground as well as in trees, where it pursues birds.

The small, oval head is hardly set off from the extremely slender body. The pupils are round and the scales keeled. The coloration varies from yellowish to olive gray, and occasionally black ones are seen. The underside of the body is very light in color. Non-experts sometimes confuse this snake with cobras since, like the cobra, it flattens its throat when excited and rises up vertically.

Demands in Captivity: Since this snake is very large and very active, it needs a big terrarium as well as a water basin of generous size. Sandy soil with some larger rocks serves well as bottom material. A hiding place underneath strips of tree bark, pieces of cork, or flat rocks and some gnarled tree limbs for climbing complete the list of necessary items. This snake needs artificial lighting all day long with sunlight or some ultraviolet lighting and air temperatures between 77° and 86°F (25°–30°C) with bottom heat warming some areas up to 90°F (32°C).

Non-Venomous Snakes and Giant Snakes and How to Keep Them

At night the temperature should drop a few degrees. These conditions are essential for the snake's well-being.

According to Trutnau, the mating period of this species extends from April to August, but depending on the geographic origin of an individual snake, mating can occur at any time of the year. The females deposit 9 to 14 eggs, and the young snakes measure 14 to 18½ inches (36–47 cm) at birth.

Indian Rat Snakes do not reproduce in captivity. They should be offered frogs, mice, sparrows, and dead fish to eat.

Hibernation: For snakes imported from the northern areas of distribution, a brief hibernating period is recommended.

Brazilian Smooth Snake   ◑ ◒

Cyclagras gigas

Length: Up to 6½ feet (2 m).

This powerful snake comes from the eastern regions of South America. Its imposing body is a golden yellow to light brown color with irregular black crossbands. It is a pleasant snake to have in a terrarium, eating small rodents like mice and rats as well as chickens, pigeons, fish, and frogs and rarely behaving aggressively toward its keeper.

In Grzimek's *Tierleben (Lives of Animals),* Reinhard and Vogel report matings that took place in August at dusk. Later the females laid up to 36 eggs around the end of October to midNovember.

The *C. gigas* has developed an interesting process to facilitate the shedding of its skin. It ties the rear portion of its body into a tight knot which it then crawls through, leaving the old skin behind rolled up in a tight ring.

Demands in Captivity: In Brazil the *C. gigas* lives in dense and impenetrable growths of cactus plants and barriguda trees. In the terrarium it should have temperatures between 68° and 82°F (20°–28°C) with 10 to 12 hours of artificial light. A number of dark hiding places and a large water basin (where the snakes sometimes linger all day long) must also be part of the setup. The snakes should not be exposed to direct sunlight.

African Egg-eating Snake   ◑ ◒

Dasypeltis scabra

Length: Up to 32 inches (80 cm).

One of the most interesting specialized eating habits among the colubrids is that of the African Egg-eating Snake, a great favorite of terrarium enthusiasts. (The Indian Egg-eating Snake, *Elachistadon westermanni,* has developed a similar technique.) The *Dasypeltis scabra* is found in dry forests and bushy areas from southern Morocco down to the tropical southern regions of Africa. The head of this slender snake is barely set off from the body although it can fit such proportionally huge bites as an unbroken small chicken egg into its mouth. The coloration is very attractive. Along the back and sides, dark patches stand out against the yellowish to light brown ground color. The scales are strongly keeled, and the elongated pupils of the eyes are vertical, giving rise to the impression that this might be a venomous snake.

The eating technique of this snake deserves a brief description. The mouth and throat are capable of incredible, almost frightening distension when the snake is about to swallow an egg. The snake's mouth literally engulfs the egg, which, because the snake has practically no teeth, moves toward the throat whole. There, rasp-like extensions of the twenty-fourth to the thirtieth vertebrae break the egg shell, and all its contents flow into

Non-Venomous Snakes and Giant Snakes and How to Keep Them

the stomach without waste. The leftover shell is then regurgitated.

Demands in Captivity: If you have a ready supply of small bird eggs, keeping an Egg-eating Snake in a terrarium presents no problem. Since it is active during the day and at dusk, some areas of the bottom should be warmed by bottom heat up to 90°F (32°C), but there should also be cooler areas, some as low as 68°F (20°C), and nighttime temperatures should drop to about the same level. The terrarium can be set up as a dry terrarium with some climbing branches and plants. The bottom should be covered with loose sand and gravel with some flat rocks to provide hiding places. The small water basin should always be filled with fresh drinking water. Occasional sunshine or ultraviolet light is important. Klingelhöffer describes the threatening posture of the *D. scabra* as follows: The snake forms itself into a coil, raises its head while flattening the sides of the neck, and opens its mouth so wide that the blackish mucous membranes inside become clearly visible.

Boa Constrictor (photo, page 63) ◐ ◒

Boa constrictor (various subspecies)

Length: 10 to 16½ feet (3–5 m).

The Boa Constrictor is well known not only among herpetologists but also among the general public partly because of the role it plays in myths, folklore, and adventure tales and partly because of its beauty and elegance. Unfortunately it sometimes suffers the fate of an involuntary guinea pig when novice snake keepers choose it as the first subject on which to practice their art. Baby Boas, which are born alive and measure about 16 inches (40 cm) at birth, look very pretty indeed. The markings, which range in color from copper and reddish brown to yellowish brown, grayish beige, and orange, make even older specimens look very attractive. In addition, these snakes, especially younger ones, are almost always peaceful and reluctant to bite.

Eight subspecies of the Boa Constrictor range from southern Mexico and some of the Caribbean islands as far south as Argentina. In some South American countries they are unfortunately hunted to supply ingredients for "healing potions." Characteristic of this species is the strong triangular head that stands out from the rest of the body. Coloration varies considerably among the subspecies and even among individual snakes from reddish brown and reddish gray to yellowish, orange, and, sometimes, dark brown hues. The markings on the back consist of light and dark spots that sometimes take on a strong orange red color toward the tail. A dark band reaches from the tip of the snout across the eyes to the throat, and the belly is a dark cream color.

One way for the novice herpetologist to distinguish boas from pythons, both of which are among the largest snakes in the world, is to know that members of the subfamily *Boidae*, unlike snakes of the subfamily *Pythonidae*, do not have lip pits. Snakes of both groups have anal spurs, a memento of earlier evolutionary stages in the form of vestigial pelvic and associated bones.

Demands in Captivity: The fact that the Boa Constrictor occurs over such a large area with very different climatic conditions indicates that there cannot be one set of rules for the temperature needs of this species. The best solution is probably to have areas of different temperatures in the terrarium with the coolest point, perhaps a shady corner, at about 72°F (22°C). Then there should be warmer places ranging up to about 95°F (35°C). There should be a slight temperature

69

Non-Venomous Snakes and Giant Snakes and How to Keep Them

difference between day and night. Adequate humidity should be maintained but without the bottom being wet. Boa Constrictors like to frequent a water basin, but it should be one that is easy to keep clean. The floor can consist simply of bare dry stone that can be heated. Or the floor can be covered with a mixture of sand and gravel. There should also be some pipes large enough for the snake to hide in. Place them so that you can glance into them easily to check on your snake. Strong, forked tree limbs are an absolute must in the terrarium of a Boa Constrictor. Depending on the snake's size, it can be fed live mammals of small to medium size and bred for laboratory purposes, such as mice, rats, guinea pigs, rabbits, chickens, and pigeons, which the snake will kill by constriction.

Rainbow Boa (photo on back cover)

Epicrates cenchria

Length: 10 to 12½ feet (3–3.8 m).
  One of the most beautifully colored boas is the Rainbow Boa with its red, blue, and brown markings, which, right after the snake has sloughed off its old skin, gleam with an iridescence reminiscent of a rainbow. This arboreal snake is found from Costa Rica down to Argentina.
Demands in Captivity: The terrarium should be set up as for a Green Tree Boa. The Rainbow Boa, which is active at dusk, prefers temperatures between 72° and 82°F (20°–28°C) with a cooler period at night but no less than 72°F (22°C). These relatively peaceful and easygoing snakes can be fed rats, mice, guinea pigs, and chicks. They are well suited to terrarium life, and they can be bred in captivity. The young are born after an incubation period of about five months and measure 20 to 25 inches (50–65 cm).

Bahaman Boa

Epicrates striatus

Length: 10 to 12 feet (3–3.5 m).
  Bahaman Boas occur on the island of Hispaniola and in the Bahamas. This snake's body is never as stout as that of other boas of comparable length. The head is clearly set off from the body, and the coloration is gray-brown to copper brown with irregular markings on the back and the sides. Between the markings, some of which fade into each other, run lighter crossbands. The head is a uniform gray. Gray is also the color of the belly, but there it is speckled with dark spots. Normally, the Bahaman Boa is easy to keep and feeds readily. It is a true tree dweller and likes to spend its time among dense branches.
Demands in Captivity: The terrarium should offer an abundance of climbing opportunities. The terrarium is set up as for the Green Tree Boa. The atmosphere should be humid and warm with temperatures between 72° and 82°F (22°–28°C) with a drop at night down to 65°F (18°C). The Bahaman Boa is active at dusk and at night and prefers small prey such as mice and young rats. It is viviparous.
Hibernation: The snake may hibernate from December to January at about 41° to 43°F (5°–6°C).

Garden Tree Boa (photo, page 64)

Corallus enydris

Length: Up to 8 feet (2.5 m).
  This is a relatively savage snake that likes to bite and is easily aroused to anger. It has a very slender body, and the head is well set off from it. The ground color ranges from brown to gray and grayish green with dark

Non-Venomous Snakes and Giant Snakes and How to Keep Them

spots along the dorsal line that may form a zigzag pattern. This snake is widely distributed in South America and inhabits primarily dense tree tops and bushes in tropical forests.
Demands in Captivity: The required temperature is about 72° to 86°F (26°–30°C) with a possible drop as low as 68°F (20°C) at night. This snake is active at dusk and at night and eats mice, rats, and birds. Since the Garden Tree Boa likes to climb in trees, the terrarium should be taller than it is wide and may be planted with epithytes and philodendrons. Breeding this snake in captivity seems to be unproblematic and has been accomplished a number of times by amateur herpetologists.

Emerald Tree Boa (photo, page 63)

Corallus caninus

Length: Over 6 feet (2 m); at most, 10 feet (3 m).

At first glance, this snake is easily confused with the *Chondropython viridis,* which is also green. Ways to distinguish the two snakes from each other are given on page 75. The most obvious of these marks is that the Emerald Tree Boa has pits on the upper lip. However, this snake is not recommended for the novice snake keeper, since feeding it—it likes small birds, such as chicks, sparrows, etc.—may at first present difficulties. Snakes of this species are usually quite peaceful in a terrarium, though they can inflict a serious bite when annoyed. Feeding primarily on birds, this snake has large and strong frontal teeth to penetrate through the feathers. The Emerald Tree Boa inhabits the dense forests of South America and, being an excellent climber, lives primarily in the tree tops. But it is also a good swimmer and benefits from having a large water basin in the terrarium.

Demands in Captivity: There should be plenty of tree limbs with lots of branches on them in the large, well ventilated terrarium. Plants are also recommended and look decorative. The bottom should consist of the same materials as for the *Chondropython viridis* (page 75). The Emerald Tree Boa needs temperatures between 79° and 86°F (26°–30°C) during the day and 68° to 75°F (20°–24°C) at night. Some exposure to ultraviolet light is recommended.

This species lives primarily on birds, but you can try feeding it small mammals.

Javelin Sand Boa (photo, page 64)

Eryx jaculus

Length: Up to 2½ feet (80 cm).

The Javelin Sand Boa is the only boa that is found in Europe, and it is found in Western Greece, the Balkan peninsula, on the Cyclades, and in Turkey, from where it spreads throughout northern Africa and as far as western Asia.
Demands in Captivity: The terrarium should simulate desert conditions and have a thick layer of sand at the bottom that is heated up to different degrees in different spots, ranging from 68° to 95°F (20°–35°C), so that the snakes can seek out the temperature they are most comfortable at. These yellowish brown snakes are quite handsome to behold, but unfortunately one rarely gets a chance to get a good look at them. To remedy this condition you can place plastic pipes that are cut in half against the glass walls of the terrarium. The snakes like to crawl into them, and then you will be able to study them. Otherwise they burrow into the sand with only the nose and eyes peeping out. These snakes are very good eaters and consume other reptiles

as well as mice. They also like reptile eggs and, occasionally, slugs.

They capture their prey by darting out of the sand and coiling their bodies around the victim.

Anaconda

Eunectes murinus

Length: 20 to 26 feet (6–8 m).

This largest of the giant serpents occurs in northeastern South America where it inhabits the tropical forests of the Amazon and Orinoco basins. There are reports of an *Eunectes murinus gigas* that measured a record length of 37½ feet (11.4 m). This amphibious snake is active more at dusk than during the night. Although it adjusts quite well to terrarium life and is peaceful, it can, when aroused to anger, be an aggressive biter.

The longish head is set off only slightly from the neck. The ground color is olive green to gray green, and there are darker spots along the back that sometimes merge into each other. A light colored stripe bordered with black runs from the eyes to the corners of the mouth. The stomach is light gray to yellowish with black spots.

A related species, the Yellow Anaconda *(Eunectes notaeus)* is smaller and lacks this light stripe.

Demands in Captivity: An effort should be made to duplicate this snake's natural environment by including, in a large terrarium containing sturdy tree limbs and rocks, a water basin that takes up at least a third of the total area. The air temperature should range between 75° and a maximum of 86°F (24°–30°C), and the water should be just a few degrees cooler. Periodic exposure to sunlight is a good idea.

The Anaconda should not be combined with other reptiles, including other giant serpents, since it may well overpower and eat them. Unlike other giant serpents, the Anaconda will feed on cold-blooded creatures and reptiles, and there are reports of Anacondas attacking and killing even crocodiles and other giant serpents. The feeding plan for the Anaconda is the same as for the Boa Constrictor (page 70). In addition, it can be fed fish. Anacondas are viviparous.

Mating is said to occur frequently in water. After a gestation period of about 230 days, the female gives birth to baby snakes measuring about 2½ feet (75 cm) and weighing about a half-pound (250 g).

Indian Python (photo, page 64)

Python molurus

Length: Up to 21 feet (6.5 m).

Most people are familiar with the looks of the Indian Python from pictures of Indian snake dancers or snake charmers. This is the largest of the pythons, and it occurs in two subspecies, the lighter colored *P. molurus molurus* and the *P. molurus bivittatus*. The latter, which occurs from Indochina to southern China, Malaysia, the Celebes, and Sumbawa, differs from its lighter relatives living on the Indian peninsula and Ceylon by not having spots with a light middle area on the sides. This darker subspecies can reach a length of up to 21 feet (6.5 m) and a weight of about 200 pounds (90 kg). The *P. molurus clearly differs from the Python regius* and the *Python curtus* by its much larger size, and the two upper lip shields with pit-like indentations also aid in distinguishing it from the *Python reticulatus.*

If you manage to breed the Indian Python in captivity, you will have one of the most

Non-Venomous Snakes and Giant Snakes and How to Keep Them

exciting experiences a terrarium keeper can have as you watch it care for its eggs. I have observed it removing infertile or underdeveloped eggs from the rest of the clutch. For the entire 60-day incubation period, the *Python molurus* stays with the eggs, with its body coiled around them, and you can see the muscle spasms that run down the body continually and make it possible for the snake to keep its body temperature as much as 13°F (7°C) above the temperature of the environment. In this way the mother protects and warms the eggs until they hatch, exhibiting, in this process, a brood behavior that is unique among reptiles. In its natural habitat the *P. molurus* inhabits dense forests in humid climates.

Demands in Captivity: To reflect the natural conditions this snake comes from, the terrarium should have a large water basin with warmed water. It goes without saying that the large tree limbs needed for a snake of this size must be strong and securely installed. The air temperature needs to be around 75° to 86°F (24°-30°C) and the water temperature should lie just a little below that. The humidity should be high, as it is in the native climate of this snake. Like most giant serpents, the Black-tailed Python is active at dusk and at night and should be fed shortly after the terrarium lights have been turned off. The food to be offered is the same as that described for the Boa Constrictor (page 70).

Reticulate Python (photo on inside front cover) ●○

Python reticulatus

Length: In exceptional cases, up to 33 feet (10 m).

The Reticulate Python occurs in Southeast Asia, in the Philippines, and on the Lesser Sunda islands. Along with the Anaconda, it is one of the world's largest serpents. Its strikingly handsome pattern of brownish yellow to reddish markings interwoven on a light ground make it a sought-after favorite for terrarium use.

But caution is in order with larger specimens because they are usually quite aggressive. They can leap to a height and distance of five feet when they attack.

Demands in Captivity: Active primarily at dusk and at night, the Reticulate Python prefers a biotope resembling that of the humid primordial forests of the tropics. The air should therefore be very humid and the terrarium very large. Younger animals like to climb on tree limbs whereas the large full-grown ones are generally found on the ground. The temperature should range between 75° and 90°F (24°-32°C). A large, built-in water basin is essential, and the water temperature should be about 79°F (26°C).

The food should consist of mammals and birds of a size appropriate to the size of the specific snake.

The Reticulate Python, like the Anaconda, should be kept singly. This species has been successfully reproduced in captivity. Trutnau had a female measuring over 16 feet (5 m) that produced 45 eggs four months after an observed mating in early December. It immediately coiled itself around the eggs. Trutnau did not observe the muscle spasms typical of other brooding pythons. After incubation at 83° to 90°F (28°-32°C), the first snakes hatched in mid-June measuring about 30 inches (75 cm) and had grown as large as 50 inches (1.3 m) by the age of three months.

Non-Venomous Snakes and Giant Snakes and How to Keep Them

Ball or **Royal Python** (photos, pages 35 and 64) ◑ ⊕

Python regius

Length: Up to 6½ feet (2 m).

The Ball Python is very handsomely marked and is one of the gentlest of the giant serpents. Its tapering head is markedly set off from the sturdy, short-tailed body. The ground color is a chocolate brown, and there are irregular light patches on the sides. A yellow band runs across the temples from the neck to the tip of the nose. Beneath this is a black band that reaches to the corners of the mouth. The abdomen is cream-colored. The area of distribution reaches from western to central Africa, where the Ball Python lives in savannas and dry forests. When the Ball Python is bothered or feels threatened, it rolls itself into a tight ball that is impossible to pull apart and keeps its head and neck tucked inside. It looks very graceful when resting in the branches of a tree. Here, too, it coils its body up in similar fashion, but the head and about one-fourth of the body rise up out of the ball. From this position, the snake lunges out at prey with lightning-like speed and sometimes swallows it while hanging in the air. The Ball Python's favorite quarry are running and jumping mice. It is more active at dusk than during the day.

Demands in Captivity: This snake prefers a temperature range of 79° to 90°F (26°–32°C) and benefits from basking in the sun. This species, too, has reproduced in captivity. Mating in February or March is followed in March to May by the laying of eggs. The 6 to 8 rather large eggs (about 3 × 2 inches [7 × 5 cm]) are usually deposited at night and stick together. The Ball Python cares for the eggs during the incubation period of about 100 days, and the young measure from 9 to 17 inches (23–43 cm) at birth.

Blood Python (photo, page 64) ● ○

Python curtus

Length: Up to 10 feet (3 m).

Because of its bright reddish brown coloring and its short, stout body, the *Python curtus* is unlikely to be mistaken for any other giant serpent. The pointed head is clearly set off from the body, and the tail is short. The upper side of the body is marked with irregular yellowish gray spots and bands that fade into each other. The head is dark with a dorsal midline, and a light line runs from behind the eye to the corner of the mouth. This species is native to Malaysia, Borneo, and Sumatra, and it lives near bodies of water in sparse forests. It is also frequently found in the water. These snakes are active at dusk and at night, and they are said to be quite aggressive and mean.

Demands in Captivity: These snakes need daytime air temperatures of about 83° to 90°F (28°–32°C) and water that is slightly cooler. A stable water basin is essential because these snakes sometimes feed in the water. A drop in temperature at night and occasional opportunities for sunning should be provided. Follow the directions given for Anacondas for preparing the bottom of the terrarium (page 72). These snakes have been successfully bred in captivity. The female looks after the brood by coiling iself around the eggs and exhibits the typical muscle spasms described above. The ideal incubation temperature is 86° to 90°F (30°–32°C), and when the young hatch after about 70 days they are about 16 inches (40 cm) long.

Non-Venomous Snakes and Giant Snakes and How to Keep Them

Green Python (photos on back cover and on page 18) ◐ ◉

Chondropython viridis

Length: Up to about 6½ feet (2 m).

This species is native to the Cape York peninsula of Australia and to New Guinea. It is very easily confused by the novice herpetologist with the *Corallus caninus* (page 71). The species under discussion here is characterized by smaller scales on the upper side of the head. The indented scales of the upper lip also help to distinguish between the two snakes. In the *Chondropython,* indentations are present only in the upper rows of the scales on the upper lip. In the *Corallus,* the indentations appear on all the scales of the upper lip. A third difference is that in the *Chondropython* the lower edge of the eye is directly adjacent to the supralabialia (upper lip scales), whereas in the *Corallus* the eye and the supralabialia are separated by small scales.

Demands in Captivity: Sturdy plants such as philodendrons can be included in the terrarium and provide an attractive background for this green snake, which usually lies draped over a branch of a stable climbing tree. Since the atmosphere in the terrarium has to be hot and humid, a mixture of sand and peat moss, as used in hydrocultures, makes a good bottom material, but it should not be too moist. A heated but not too large water basin and temperatures between 72° to 92°F (22°–33°C) during the day and 68° to 77°F (20°–25°C) at night are required.

The young of this species with their generally yellowish or reddish coloration and bluish markings are particularly attractive.

Rock Python ◑ ◖ ◎

Python sebae

Length: Up to 20 feet (6 m).

This strong and very lively snake with a reputation for being quite ferocious occurs in the southern and tropical regions of Africa and as far north as the southern rim of the Sahara. Its ground color ranges from light brown to grayish brown with black brown or red brown patches on the back and crescent-shaped marks with light centers on the sides. Because of these markings it is sometimes called the Hieroglyph Snake. It is by no means true that all Rock Pythons are vicious; some have become quite good pets that are easy to take care of.

Demands in Captivity: Accustomed to open plains, thick grass, and low bushes, this snake prefers a rather dry atmosphere in the terrarium. But it should have a fair-sized water basin, of which it will make frequent use. The dry bottom material may consist of mixed sand and gravel, though some keepers of giant serpents recommend the more sterile conditions provided by a flat floor that is easy to keep clean. Of course, the snakes need refuges that should be open to inspection by the keeper. Daytime air temperatures should be between 77° and 90°F (25°–32°C), and at night it can be as cool as 65°F (18°C). These snakes can be fed mice, rats, hamsters, rabbits, guinea pigs, and all kinds of poultry. In its native habitat the Rock Python hibernates for two to four months. It lays 30 to 50 (sometimes as many as 100) leathery eggs measuring about 3½ × 5 inches (9 × 16 cm) from which the 24- to 28-inch (60–70 cm) long baby snakes hatch after about 3 months.

Non-Venomous Snakes and Giant Snakes and How to Keep Them

Burrowing Python ◑ ◔

Calabaria reinhardtii

Length: Up to 40 inches (100 cm).

This is the only subterranean giant serpent living in western Africa. Its small head, perfectly round body, smooth scales, and short tail are clear signs of its burrowing way of life. The back of the body is black-brown with brick red and light spots. The head and tail are almost black. The underside is brown or gray and has yellow or brown spots similar to those on the back. This python lives in tropical forests where it likes to hide in the loose soil or in the burrows of rodents.

Demands in Captivity: The setup of the terrarium should reflect the natural living conditions of this burrowing snake. There should be pieces of bark, slabs of wood, loose, sandy soil, and a water basin. Although the *Calabaria* likes to dig in the soil, it occasionally makes use of climbing limbs in the terrarium. Contrary to reports by other authorities, the specimen that I had accepted food readily and would eat mice fed to it by hand. It would press its prey against the terrarium floor or wall with its body to kill it. I kept the snake with good results at 83°F (28°C) during the day and 72°F (22°C) at night. Ordinary artificial lighting seems to be sufficient. Although this peaceable snake never tries to bite and, when frightened, rolls itself up into a ball, tucking its head inside, the natives are much afraid of it and think it has two heads. Unfortunately, much too little is known about the biology of this beautiful and interesting snake and the requirements for keeping it in captivity. About its reproductive habits, we merely know that it lays eggs and that the clutch is small.

Black-headed Python (photo, page 64) ● ◔

Aspidites melanocephalus

Length: Up to 9 feet (2.8 m).

This Australian snake has to be counted among the most beautiful giant serpents. Its head and neck are set off against the light brown body by its glossy black color. Darker crossbands grace the body, and the abdomen is cream-colored. Not much is known about the habits of this splendid snake which, because of its high price, is seldom seen in terrariums.

Demands in Captivity: To meet the demands of this ground-dwelling snake, the large dry terrarium should have a hard, rocky bottom and contain a small to medium-sized water basin. The Black-headed Python needs air temperature of between 77° and 86°F (25°–30°C) with a nighttime drop of about 9°F (5°C). It can be fed mice, rats, and birds.

Protected Snake Species

The Washington Convention on International Trade in Endangered Species of Wild Fauna and Flora includes several species of snakes in its Appendix I (species in danger of immediate extinction) and Appendix II (threatened, but not in immediate danger of extinction). There are three ways of legally buying or trading species listed in this document.

• Species listed in Appendix I or II can be legally kept if you have proof that the snake was imported before the Washington Convention went into effect.

• Species listed in Appendix I may be kept if you have a document from the country of origin stating that the specimens in question as well as their parents were born in captivity.

• For species listed in Appendix II, you have to be able to present an export permit issued by the snake's country of origin.

If you buy a snake, the dealer has to supply you with a copy of the export permit so that you can prove that you acquired your snake in conformance with the requirements of the Washington Convention.

Appendix I includes the following snake species:
Epicrates inornatus inornatus
Epicrates subflavus
Python molurus molurus

Appendix II lists the following:
All pythons not listed in Appendix I.
Epicrates cenchria cenchria
Boa constrictor constrictor
Eunectes notaeus
Cyclagras gigas
Pseudoboa clelia clelia
Elachistodon westermanni
Thamnophis elegans hammondi

Organizations Concerned with Snakes

American Society of Ichthyologists
   and Herpetologists
United States National Museum
Washington, DC 20560

Herpetology League
University of Oklahoma
Box 478
Oklahoma City, OK 73111

Society for the Study of Amphibians
   and Reptiles
Zoology Department
Ohio University
Athens, OH 45701

Barron's Complete Pet Care Library

Pet Owner's Manuals
African Gray Parrots
Amazon Parrots
Bantams
Beagles
Beekeeping
Boxers
Canaries
Cats
Chinchillas
Chow-Chows
Cockatiels
Dachshunds
Doberman Pinschers
Dwarf Rabbits
Fancy Pigeons
Feeding and Sheltering
   European Birds
Ferrets
Gerbils
German Shepherds
Golden Retrievers
Goldfish
Guinea Pigs
Hamsters
Labrador Retrievers
Lizards in the Terrarium

Long-Haired Cats
Lovebirds
Mice
Mutts
Mynahs
Nonvenomous Snakes
Parakeets
Parrots
Ponies
Poodles
Rabbits
Schnauzers
Sheep
Snakes
Spaniels
Tropical Fish
Turtles
Zebra Finches

Cat Fancier's Series
Burmese Cats
Longhair Cats
Siamese Cats

Training Guide
Communicating with Your Dog

New Pet Handbooks
New Bird Handbook
New Cat Handbook
New Aquarium Fish Handbook
New Dog Handbook
New Duck Handbook
New Finch Handbook
New Goat Handbook
New Parakeet Handbook
New Parrot Handbook
New Softbill Handbook
New Terrier Handbook

New Premium Series
Aquarium Fish Survival Manual
Cat Care Manual
Complete Book of Budgerigars
Complete Book of Parrots
Dog Care Manual
Goldfish and Ornamental Carp
Horse Care Manual
Labyrinth Fish

First Aid for Pets
First Aid for Your Cat
First Aid for Your Dog

Index

Index